25
YEARS
OF THE
RED
ARROWS

25 YEARS OF THE RED ARROWS

Squadron Leader Tim Miller

Ray Hanna

Arthur Gibson

STANLEY PAUL

London Sydney Auckland Johannesburg

Proceeds to The Red Arrows Trust

Stanley Paul & Co. Ltd
An imprint of Random Century Ltd
20 Vauxhall Bridge Road, London SW1V 2SA
Random Century Australia (Pty) Ltd
20 Alfred Street, Milsons Point, Sydney, NSW 2061
Random Century New Zealand Limited
PO Box 40–086, Glenfield, Auckland 10
Century Hutchinson South Africa (Pty) Ltd
PO Box 337, Bergvlei 2012, South Africa
First published 1990
© Text Diana Woolley 1990
© Photographs Arthur Gibson 1990
Designed by Roger Walker
Set in Century Old Style by Tek Art Ltd
Printed and bound by New Interlitho, Milan, Italy
British Library Cataloguing in Publication Data

ISBN 0 09 174446 6

HALF TITLE:
The 1968 Gnat Team over the White Cliffs of Dover in 'Big
Arrow' formation

FRONTISPIECE:
A Synchro-break above the 'Big Seven' formation over RAF
Kemble in 1980

TITLE PAGE:
Left: The Crest of the Royal Air Force Central Flying School
Right: The Royal Air Force Aerobatic Team's Official Squadron
Badge

CONTENTS

INTRODUCTION
ARTHUR GIBSON

It is twenty-five years since the Red Arrows were formed. They are sometimes referred to as the 'premier aerobatic team of the Royal Air Force' or as the 'RAF's leading aerobatic team' or as the 'British Air Force official aerobatic team'. These are well-meant descriptions, all of them, but all are wrong. The truth is really much simpler: since 1965, the Red Arrows have been *the* Aerobatic Team of the Royal Air Force.

There are, of course, other flying display teams in the RAF, all with some sort of official standing. Normally they represent a particular station or unit. Only the Red Arrows, however, represent the whole of the Royal Air Force – and that means that, at international displays, they represent Britain.

The Arrows are, in fact, unique in a number of ways. For instance, it was only when they were formed that the RAF had an aerobatic team whose full-time job was display flying. Before that, the chosen team was usually drawn from an operational squadron of Fighter Command, and its display function was secondary to its operational duty.

I have been highly privileged because since my first encounter with the Arrows in 1967 I have flown with almost every Team. I have made three films about them and taken a very great many photographs. For me it all began in that year when I was a consultant to the then British Aircraft Corporation. I was at Le Bourget for the Paris Airshow where BAC was promoting the Aloha One-Eleven. It was a stylish blue, gold and white and it struck me what a lovely contrast it made to the red Gnats. I therefore approached the Team Leader and suggested that we might fix up a formation on the way back to England.

After an initial mini-skirmish (only of words, I hasten to state) which lasted a couple of days – during which, as I later discovered, the Team Leader was checking out my credentials and capabilities – the idea was accepted. As a result, I took my first photographs of the One-Eleven with seven Gnats from the eighth, spare Gnat (the Arrows were not yet displaying nine aircraft). And thus an enduring relationship had begun.

The 1970 Gnat Team in 'Feathered Arrow'

In 1967 it was suggested that I should make a film of the Arrows, which proved to be very successful. This venture was repeated in 1980 when I made a second film, this time featuring the Hawk (an aircraft from which it is much harder to film and photograph than from a Gnat).

Having, to date, photographed the Red Arrows in all but their first two display seasons, I have clearly experienced many memorable occasions and produced some photographs to commemorate them. Obvious highlights were the formation with Concorde and the fly-past in honour of the Queen's Silver Jubilee.

One of the aspects of the Red Arrows which I believe to be undervalued is their status as unpaid overseas super-salesmen of the aeroplanes they fly. We will probably never appreciate the debt which the British aerospace industry owes to the Red Arrows through their natural capacity to 'sell' the product they demonstrate. Of course, this is not the reason that they display, any more than is the clear recruiting appeal that their performances have. Nevertheless, I do not believe that it is mere coincidence that this country has obtained contracts for aerospace products from certain overseas countries not long after they have been visited by the Team.

In the next section of this book, Ray Hanna writes about the history of the Red Arrows and supplies some background information on the way the Team flies. Following this, Tim Miller, Arrows Leader 1988–90, describes current Arrows operational methods. Ray flew in Gnats while Tim now flies in Hawks but (as I can personally verify, having flown in the back seats of both) the background flying details given by Ray apply equally to both aircraft.

Air Marshal Sir Ivor Broom became Commandant of the Central Flying School when Ray Hanna was in his last full season as Red Arrows Leader, and he has described him in the following words:

> [Ray Hanna] epitomised all the qualities which one looks for in an aerobatic team leader. An outstanding pilot with several thousand hours' flying on a wide variety of aircraft. Firm and decisive in his orders. A leader in every sense of the word. A man others would follow without question, for he led by example.
>
> He demanded the highest form of self discipline from his men. They responded so magnificently that he built the Red Arrows into the most famous formation aerobatic team in Europe – and probably in the world.

The reason that Ray has joined with me in the preparation of this book is that it was he with whom I had the verbal skirmish at Le Bourget in 1967. Since then I have enjoyed not only a continuing association with the Red Arrows, but also a continuing friendship with Ray.

Photographs spanning twenty-three years... The 1967 Gnat Team escorting the World's first short-haul jet liner, the BAC One-Eleven. The Hawks of the 1989 Team 'formating' on the fastest British Rail diesel-electric high speed train, aptly named by Her Majesty The Queen Mother in November 1989... 'The Red Arrow'

THE EARLY YEARS
RAY HANNA

In 1964 it was planned to include in the SBAC Show at Farnborough an hour-long Royal Air Force contribution. In addition to the Red Pelicans of the Central Flying School, therefore, it was decided to form a second formation aerobatics team within RAF Flying Training Command. This team was based at No 4 Flying Training School at Valley on the Isle of Anglesey and consisted of five Hawker Siddeley Gnats flying as the 'Yellowjacks' under the leadership of Flight Lieutenant Lee Jones. This team was effectively the embryo of the Red Arrows.

The No 4 FTS team owed its formation almost solely to the personal initiative and enthusiasm of Lee Jones. Then thirty-six, he was a very experienced fighter pilot who had recently begun instructing. He had first led an aerobatics team when he headed the formation put up by Fighter Command Operational Conversion Unit at RAF Chivenor in 1958–9, and in 1960 he had become a member of the Black Arrows. This was a team flying all-black Hawker Hunters which from 1957 had been the premier jet aerobatics team of the Royal Air Force.

To skilled and experienced instructors with a fighter-pilot background, the Gnat (which had then been in use at RAF Valley for only about a year) had come as a welcome and refreshing development in the equipment used for the advanced flying phase of instruction. It would have been surprising if Lee Jones – with his enthusiasm for formation aerobatics already fired – had not itched for an opportunity to exploit the speed, exceptional manoeuvrability and precision of this lively newcomer to the aerobatics scene. The formation of the Yellowjacks (the name was originally simply a call-sign) was very much his personal achievement; he conceived the idea, put it forward, and was instrumental in getting it accepted.

Looking back it may seem odd that there should ever have been doubts about the 'rightness' of the Gnat for the aerobatics role. Remember, though, that the plane was then very new to service and, like almost every new aircraft, had its share of teething troubles. When a new aircraft represents as big an advance over its predecessors as the Gnat did, personnel as well as equipment frequently need a 'shakedown' period.

'Diamond Nine' – the basic Red Arrows formation – photographed from No 2 on the downswing of the arrival loop at sunset at Nice

Squadron Leader Ray Hanna, the longest serving Leader in the history of the Team... four years from 1966 to 1969

From many points of view there was that sense of 'rightness' about the Gnat from the very start. For one thing it was a good-looking aircraft, and that is not as unimportant in the context of formation aerobatics as some might think. More importantly, it had the handiness and accuracy of control which make possible slick changes of formation and the precision flying so essential for display work when the aircraft must operate fairly near the ground at relatively high speeds. All this, plus unsurpassed swept-wing manoeuvrability, made the Gnat the ideal compromise between the powerful fighters of earlier years and the slower, less sprightly trainers which had temporarily filled the gap.

The success of the Yellowjacks brought this home, and official recognition of the fact soon followed. In 1965 the ten Gnats were formally established as the full-time Royal Air Force aerobatics team, operating under the immediate command of the CFS. The 'Red Arrows era' had begun.

Opposite: The Yellowjacks of No 4 FTS RAF Valley, forerunners of the Red Arrows, and (inset) the Red Pelicans, the jet aerobatic team of Central Flying School

The name itself was officially chosen, unlike the titles of some earlier teams which had begun as purely unofficial nicknames in press reports and elsewhere. The title of the team which the Gnats took over – the Red Pelicans – had entirely logical origins: the aircraft had a red paint-scheme, and there is a pelican depicted in the official crest of the CFS. When the new CFS team was formed, the red finish was retained for the aircraft to maintain continuity of CFS's aerobatics teams, and it was therefore logical that 'Red' should form part of the title. 'Arrows' not only suited the style of the Gnat but also gave a link with the most famous of recent Royal Air Force aerobatics teams, the Black Arrows.

The Red Arrows were based at Kemble in Gloucestershire. This deliberate separation of the Team from the main CFS establishment at Little Rissington reflected official policy towards display aerobatics. There were to be no half-measures: the Team's sole responsibility was to be formation aerobatics displays, with no other commitments to compromise the efficient discharge of this duty.

A thorough job was made of setting up the Team for its new full-time aerobatics role, although for the first four years it functioned on a year-to-year basis with personnel loaned or seconded from other units. A Team Manager was appointed to take overall command of the unit, with responsibility for administration and for making detailed arrangements for the season's programme. He also acted as the Team's commentator at air shows. Later, when the Team Leader was in overall command, the Team Manager's function became almost exclusively an administrative one, but he continued to act as commentator and 'ferry pilot' for the tenth Gnat. In many ways, the Team Manager has always been the most hard-worked member of the Team.

An Engineering Officer was also appointed to take charge of the ground support teams, and in 1967 the Arrows were given their own Team Adjutant. Then in 1969 the Team was established on a permanent basis as the equivalent of a standard Royal Air Force squadron.

The Red Arrows' first public appearance was in May 1965 at the Biggin Hill International Air Fair. Success was immediate and sixty shows were flown in that first season. An indication of the initial impact made by the Team can be gained from the fact that in March 1966 they were honoured with the Royal Aero Club's major award, the Britannia Trophy.

In the 1966 and 1967 seasons, when I had taken over the leadership from Lee Jones, the number of shows in which we took part rose to between eighty and ninety. In most respects, though, our vintage year was 1968 – the Royal Air Force's fiftieth anniversary year – when we gave no less than ninety-eight displays. We should undoubtedly have topped a hundred but for the cancellation of some overseas shows. In a similar year it is estimated that something like two and a quarter million people see the Red Arrows 'in the flesh'. Even that figure is minimal, however, in comparison with the numbers who see the Team on television through live and recorded coverage of shows such as Farnborough and Biggin Hill.

The Black Arrows – the first jet aerobatic team to attract public attention

Far left: One of the best known international venues in the world, SBAC's Farnborough Airshow. Here the 1982 Team pass over the enormous marquees which house the static exhibitions and manufacturer's hospitality suites. *Above:* In contrast the 1968 Biggin Hill Air Fair which typifies the showbiz atmosphere attended by the general public. *Left:* Le Bourget 1969 when the Paris Air Show drew its record crowd partly due to Concorde 001 making its public debut

Competition between the leading teams at international shows is friendly but fierce. Obviously there can be no absolute table of merit in so subjective an affair as formation aerobatics; personal tastes and preferences must make themselves felt and, since no two teams' performances are ever identical in content or style, some spectators will inevitably prefer one, some another.

To a greater degree than any earlier or contemporary team, the Red Arrows mastered the problems of providing the spectators with a continuous, flowing spectacle. Too often the highlights in other teams' displays were achieved only at the expense of intervals of empty sky while their aircraft repositioned themselves. If there is anything in the idea that different teams reflect different aspects of national character, perhaps it is the British readiness to accept compromise that made the Arrows ready to sacrifice ideas for spectactular manoeuvres if they did not fit into the overall continuity of the display sequence. Whatever the reason, the Royal Air Force aerobatics team has not only consistently maintained the crispness and accuracy of its flying despite the demands of its long season, but has also unfailingly given performances which make their twenty-minute spot in the programme an intricate aerial ballet.

At any major air show the spectators range in knowledgeability from a small, select bunch of professional pilots who are capable of judging the finer points of flying, to families who come simply to enjoy a day out. A modern air force carries out most of its allotted tasks out of sight of the public, often beyond the borders of its home country. Air displays therefore provide the public with its only real point of contact with the Service, and for this reason it has always been the policy not only of the Red Arrows but also of the Royal Air Force as a whole to plan displays to appeal to the public rather than simply to a few connoisseurs of flying. All the same, aerobatics pilots are human enough to want also to impress their fellow professionals. A really good display satisfies both groups.

There is no particular mystery about the art of formation flying. If you take your car and try to keep formation with another – keeping station, say, exactly three feet behind it – you can do it by careful steering and judicious use of the accelerator, so long as the driver ahead of you drives smoothly and does not fool around. The same basically holds true in flying, but with the additional complication that the machines are travelling far faster and in three planes of movement instead of two.

The starting point of formation flying is two aircraft flying together. One pilot aligns his aircraft with the other and, providing the lead pilot flies smoothly, a basic formation is achieved. The formating pilot concentrates his reactions and energies on following the leader's movements, making his own aircraft as far as possible an extension of the lead machine. By adding other aircraft to this basic pair, on the wings and astern, the formation is gradually built up.

In the final analysis there are only three basic formation positions: echelon, line abreast and line astern. However many aircraft are used, all formation patterns are permutations of these three.

Echelon is the first formation for the pilot to master. The easiest way

The only occasion on which four of Europe's national teams have been photographed in the air together. Taken in Belgium (and photographed by the Belgium Air Force) it shows the teams of Italy, leading the French with the Belgium team (top) and the Red Arrows (bottom)

to explain it is to go back to the fundamental two-aircraft formation in which, in echelon, No 2 flies on the leader's right and slightly behind him, but in the same vertical plane. (If he flies slightly above the leader in the same position, then it is a stepped-up echelon.) Lateral position needs to be maintained with the minimum use of the aircraft's ailerons, and pilots should master the technique of holding echelon formation absolutely smoothly and steadily before progressing to the more difficult line-abreast formation. With line abreast, as with echelon, the first requirement is to practise in straight and level flight until accurate assessment of the spacing between the aircraft becomes almost instinctive and automatic. Only then can a pilot move on to more ambitious aerobatic manoeuvres. In line astern, the third basic formation, the following aircraft flies with its nose just behind and below the tail of the machine ahead and its fin and rudder just in the jet efflux.

The Pilots, Managers and Engineering Officers of the European national aerobatic teams, represented by the Portuguese (back left), the Swiss (back centre), the Spanish (back right), the French (centre left), and the Italians (centre right), who all displayed at the Silver Anniversary Celebrations of the Red Arrows (front centre) at their home base, RAF Scampton, on 4 October 1989

Regardless of the position a pilot is going to fly in the display, he will first have to master these three basic formations. As more aircraft are added and different permutations are built up, spacings between aircraft will vary. Maintaining evenly balanced spacing throughout the formation – whatever the number of aircraft involved and whatever the attitude in which they are flying – is the first essential for good displays.

Keeping station and distance accurately means that each pilot must have clearly defined reference points by which he can line up his machine with the next man's. When two Gnats were in echelon, for instance, the pilot in No 2 would keep station by using two imaginary reference lines on the leader's aircraft. One was a line through the triangle of the ejector-seat warning sign, just behind No 1's cockpit, and the navigation light on No 1's starboard wing-tip. The second was a line from the rear tip of the tail planc to the end of the jet pipe on No 1's aircraft. As long as No 2 kept these two sets of references lined up, a perfect echelon formation would be held by the two Gnats.

As the formation patterns grow larger and more complex, the task becomes more difficult. The leader's aircraft remains the principal reference point for every man in the formation but pilots in some positions need additional cross-references in order to hold station precisely.

It is easiest to illustrate this by reference to the 'Diamond Nine' formation, the most compact and most basic formation that can be flown by nine aircraft. Diamond Nine has two aircraft in echelon on each side of the leader, Nos 2 and 4 being on his right and Nos 3 and 5 on his left. Nos 6 and 7 fly in line astern on the leader, No 8 in line astern on No 2, and No 9 in line astern on No 3. The only way in which the pilots in the outside and rearmost positions can maintain constant steadiness of spacing in formation is by continual reference to the leader while at the same time continuing to cross-refer to the aircraft beside or in front of them, ignoring any unnecessary movements by these inboard aircraft.

This art of station-keeping is essential for good formation display flying and is something which comes only with practice and experience. To aerobatics pilots this is known as the 'finesse technique', and it can be developed only by working as a team.

The reason why this skill has to be acquired, even by expert individual pilots, through sheer hard work with the team really comes down to a fact of human nature. Put two identical aircraft together manned by pilots of identical skill, ask them to carry out a manoeuvre in unison, and however well matched the men and machines, there will always be some shifts in the position of one aircraft in relation to the other. For one thing, the air is not a constant medium; there are all sorts of variations over very small distances. If the leader's position shifts, the pilot of the second aircraft has to try to anticipate it and compensate for it almost instantaneously.

A photograph which conveys something of the tightness and precision of the Red Arrows' formation flying – the team rolling in 'Wineglass' formation, probably the most difficult formation of all to roll

Top to bottom: Start-up of the Gnat's Orpheus turbo-jet engines before marshalling the aircraft out of the pan to the taxyway prior to take-off from a wet Kemble runway.
Right: A belly-on shot taken during an 'Apollo' roll showing the clean, beautiful, swept lines of the Gnat

Squadron Leader Ray Hanna and members of the 1969 team during a briefing session at their base at Kemble

When other aircraft are added to the formation, the farther they are from the origin of the shift in position, the more they will tend to enlarge the relative movement, increasing the demand on the skill of the pilot in accepting and compensating for it. When you are flying at 350/450 mph with only a few feet between your wing-tip and the next man's, it is not human nature to accept these changes in relative position without some reaction. If your partner's aircraft edges towards you, your natural instinct is to edge away. If you do, though, you are apt to exaggerate the amount of movement. Carry that effect cumulatively through a formation of nine aircraft, and the ninth man is likely to be reacting fairly violently – 'flashing about', in fact.

The formation leader's first job, therefore, is to fly every manoeuvre as smoothly and accurately as possible. He has also to position the manoeuvres precisely within the confines of his display site and in such a way that they will be seen to the best advantage by the spectators. The more smoothly and steadily the leader flies, the easier the task of the rest of the team.

Opposite: 'Nine Arrow' formation on top of a loop

Obviously, if there is any shift or irregularity in the leader's flying, the sooner it is damped out within the formation the better; the farther it travels, the more it will be amplified. For that reason, it is normal practice to have the most experienced pilots in the positions immediately to the left and right and astern of the leader. If all three fly smoothly and steadily, there is a solid foundation on which the rest of the formation can be built.

Accurate station-keeping is achieved solely by 'eyeball' judgement on the part of the pilots – instruments cannot help them. 'Finesse' depends very largely on building up confidence between all the members of the team and especially between the team and its leader. Without that confidence it would be impossible to relax while in formation, and this is essential because tension leads to over-controlling and fatigue.

All the leader can do is make sure that he provides as steady a reference point for his team as possible; he has to rely on them to keep station accurately. His task, in fact, is to concentrate literally on flying the whole team as one machine. For him, it feels very similar to flying a large, cumbersome, aircraft through fighter-type manoeuvres.

Like the other pilots, the leader must rely on 'eyeball' judgement for the accuracy of his flying. Instruments are used solely to achieve the desired aerobatic entry and exit speeds and to maintain the planned sequence pattern. Even then, the leader will refer only momentarily to his airspeed indicator, altimeter and engine-power instruments.

It may be thought that no experienced pilot should have much difficulty in simply flying smoothly, but it should be remembered that much of the interest in a display comes from quick changes of direction and manoeuvres which involve high g-loadings. A leader therefore has to develop the ability to compromise between the conflicting requirements of smooth flying and positive, crisp initiation of manoeuvres and changes of direction.

In more technical terms, experience shows that it is better for a leader to maintain positive g throughout the display sequence; the fewer relaxations he makes, the easier it is for the team to follow his manoeuvres. The rate at which g is applied can be crucial because a tendency to snatch or apply g abruptly can take the team unawares, causing raggedness. Pilots new to leading a formation are apt to be too gentle in the rate of application, however, and this leads to a lack of crispness in manoeuvres which tends to dull the overall performance.

Naturally, the optimum amount of g varies from one type of aircraft to another and from one kind of manoeuvre to another. With the Gnat as flown by the Red Arrows, the ideal g-loadings for loops were between 3½ and 4g, with a top limit of about 4½g, and for rolls between 2 and 2½g.

When one talks of formation aerobatic 'manoeuvres', most ordinary spectators probably think that there is an almost endless variety. In fact, just as the different formations are built up from the three basics of echelon, line abreast and line astern, so all manoeuvres are really permutations of three 'fundamentals': loop, roll and wing-over.

The 'Vixen' break over Central Flying School at Little Rissington in 1973 for the benefit of a Ministry of Defence photographer

The spectacular opposition roll of the Synchro Pair, against the backdrop of Ramsey, Isle of Man, and (inset) a cockpit view of the cross-over in the 'Roulette' manoeuvre

The loop must be the oldest of all aerobatic manoeuvres. It needs to be very precisely flown and smoothly executed if it is to be effective in formation. Initiation of the loop has to be progressive but positive, and the right degree of smoothness of entry into the manoeuvre is more easily achieved from a shallow dive than from straight and level flight. The leader's aim should be to reach maximum g-loading when 40 or 50 degrees of the loop have been completed, and back pressure should be maintained to hold just clear of the pre-stall 'nibble'. At the top of the loop it is generally necessary to ease off the back pressure, but it needs to be increased again as the formation enters the second half of the loop, with the leader aiming at a constant pull for final recovery in order to flow into the next manoeuvre.

The technique for a formation barrel roll is governed partly by the size and frontal 'spread' of the formation. Three or four compactly grouped aircraft can be rolled quite quickly without much back pressure being applied. A larger and 'wider-fronted' formation has to take it rather more slowly, with a definite back pressure being maintained throughout the manoeuvre. There is an instinctive inclination to ease off the pressure when inverted, but if the leader gives way to this temptation the wing-men will tend to be thrown or the whole formation appear 'dished'.

The wing-over, the third of the basic manoeuvres, is a combination of a loop and a turn. If the leader does not fly it correctly, he can make life very difficult for his team. Again, the most important thing for the leader to do is to avoid abrupt variations of control force; once he has set the angle of bank and pull force, he needs to keep them constant.

By judiciously juggling various permutations of the three basic formations and the three basic manoeuvres, an aerobatics team can build up a surprisingly varied display routine. However well each component formation and manoeuvre are flown, though, they will all be wasted if the whole display sequence is not presented in a manner which shows them to the best advantage and continuously maintains interest. This really comes down to the leader having his team in the right place, with the right formation, at the right time. It sounds simple, but it is in some ways the most difficult piece of technique for a new leader to master.

A number of factors need to be taken into account when it comes to this elusive question of 'presentation', but the overriding one should always be to ensure that the public can see all that is going on. Almost the first thing to determine is the datum point for the display. This is dictated mainly by the crowd line at the particular show. At many air shows, such as Paris or Farnborough, datum will almost certainly be a point opposite the President's tent, on a line running parallel with the crowd line.

The Arrows Leader's objective is to start and end each manoeuvre, or to time the highlight of it, so that it occurs exactly on the datum line. A perfectly executed formation loop, for instance, will begin and end on the datum line. The ultimate, in fact, is to present the whole sequence so that no spectator needs to turn his head more than 60 degrees to either side or raise it more than 50 degrees.

A typical 'early-in-year' training session at height over Gloucestershire

Left: The team transitting at low-level in loose battle formation along the French Riviera. *Top:* A head-on view of the Gnat fitted with slipper tanks for transit flights. *Above:* A practice nine-ship 'line astern' taken from the Manager's aircraft

In loops, the aim is to have the Team either running straight at datum point or flying directly away from it, and the datum remains the focus of the whole manoeuvre whether it is carried out at a relatively fine angle to the datum line or a relatively large one. In rolling manoeuvres, the best presentation is achieved by running parallel to the crowd, timing the roll so that the aircraft cross the datum line inverted.

Weather conditions obviously have a very great bearing on presentation. The Red Arrows have always aimed to have three basic display sequences, tailored to conditions ranging from good to just short of non-flyable. It is the Leader's decision as to which of the three shall be used. Within these three basic frameworks, however, he may also decide upon a number of minor variations in presentation. For instance, if marginal cloud conditions limit the height available, it pays to reduce the frontage of a wide formation so that a faster, flatter roll can be flown.

The biggest test of a Team's experience and resourcefulness is likely to be provided on overseas tours. It is not unusual for the Team to go into a display without having previously flown at that particular venue and with no opportunity for practice on site. The Leader then has to draw on his experience to 'feel it out' as he and the Team begin the display. To get the positioning and timing of the various manoeuvres right, he may have to be harsher than usual with control movements, tightening loops and turns. The Team learns to accept this and, with experience, can often anticipate what the Leader will want of them.

The same qualities of anticipation and swift but calculating assessment of the situation are needed all through the display season. Anticipation plays a big part in carrying out formation changes in mid-manoeuvre in such a manner that they look slick and crisp but not rushed to the ground spectator. A good deal of the continuity of interest in a display depends upon a succession of smooth changes of formation, to which the spectator's attention is usually drawn by the Team's commentator. Safety – always a top priority in display flying – as well as crispness and evenness of formation changes, demands that no move should be made without a clear-cut, readily understandable order from the Leader. It does not take long, though, for each pilot to learn to think a move ahead so that he is ready for each order even before he is given his cue.

A good many different qualities help to make up a successful formation aerobatics pilot, but anticipation and alertness are certainly among the most important of them. Without these qualities in every pilot, there must be a time lag between the giving of an order and the completion of the action it calls for. It is the elimination of those tiny delays and hesitancies which, since their first season, has made the Red Arrows perhaps the most consistently successful of all international teams.

One of the rare displays flown with slipper tanks

A photograph taken from No 8 (outside right of 'Big Nine' formation) a few minutes after flying over Buckingham Palace when the Royal Air Force saluted Her Majesty The Queen on the occasion of her Silver Jubilee in 1977. It shows Vulcans, Buccaneers, Jaguars, Victors, Lightnings, Phantoms, which, with the nine Gnats of the Red Arrows, made up this unique 25-ship formation, each aircraft representing one year of Her Majesty's reign.

Concorde 002 flown by Brian Trubshaw and John Cochrane (the first test pilots of the British programme) formate 'in-the-box' on the 1973 Gnat Team, photographed as the whole formation 'show-off' as they overfly the RAF Stations of Kemble, Brize Norton, Little Rissington and Fairford. The inset shows the UK's most popular aviation photograph – 'The Best of British' – depicting the Cunard QE2, a British Airways Concorde and the 1985 Hawk Team

THE TEAMS 1965–1989

ARTHUR GIBSON

The Red Arrows fly an average of a hundred shows a year totalling, at the time of writing, almost 2500 shows and over 7000 practice sorties.

In the following section are illustrations of all twenty-five Teams since 1965. The pictures all show the display pilots and some include the Manager and the First Line Engineering Officer, but none (except that for 1989) includes the ground crew. This is slightly regrettable because although the engineers and technicians may not be as glamorous as the men in red suits, their contribution to the Team is crucial. However, I believe that in the remainder of this book Tim Miller has gone some way towards showing how much work is put in by the ground crew (both first and second line) to keep the Hawks airworthy and thus enable the pilots to fly their enthralling displays.

Tim Miller is the eleventh Leader. His first tour with the Team was from 1982 to 1984 (when Sqn Ldr Blackwell was Boss) and he rejoined in 1988, making the jubilee year his second in the hot seat. I refer to it as a hot seat because I consider that the Leader's job is tougher now than it has ever been. The pressures within the Team are just the same as they were on day one, but now there are added political and financial pressures. Defence budgets are continually being questioned and in this context there are always those who will suggest that maintaining an aerobatics team is a waste of money, although this does not take account of the Team's value, referred to earlier. So, as well as running the Team and leading it on the ground and in the air, the Leader has to play an almost ambassadorial role in talks with politicians, officials and other influential individuals. And, of course, there is also the environmental lobby to be appeased.

In spite of all these factors, Tim Miller has never failed to maintain the consistency of performance which is the Red Arrows' perpetual aim and which, in my opinion, sometimes means that they are almost *too* good because they make it look so easy!

Having known all eleven Leaders I can confirm that they all share many similar characteristics. This is reinforced by the fact that if I were to be asked to give a brief description of Tim Miller I could not do better than to repeat the words of Air Marshal Sir Ivor Broom quoted in the Introduction. That summation of Ray Hanna applies equally to Tim Miller.

The nine-ship line-abreast, the toughest station-keeping formation to hold

1965 Leader F/L L. Jones, No 2 F/L B. A. Nice, No 3 F/L R. G. Hanna, No 4 F/L G. L. Ranscombe, No 5 F/O P. G. Hay, No 6 F/L R. E. W. Loverseed, No 7 F/L H. J. D. Prince, No 8 F/L E. C. F. Tilsley. Manager S/L R. E. Storer. Engineers F/O Harrow, F/O Whitby. *Ground Crew:* F/Sgt Hutson, Sgt Scott, Sgt Smallman, Cpl Casey, Cpl Chadburn, Cpl Fernside, Cpl Kellaher, Cpl Mayes, J/T Austin, J/T Hardgreaves, J/T Howse, J/T Hurren, J/T Mearns, SAC Arliss, SAC Boucher, SAC Dawson, SAC Gannon, SAC Green, SAC Thomas.

1966 Leader S/L R. G. Hanna, No 2 S/L D. A. Bell, No 3 S/L R. W. Langworthy, No 4 S/L P. R. Evans, No 5 S/L R. Booth, No 6 S/L H. J. D. Prince, No 7 F/L T. J. G. Nelson, No 8 F/L F. J. Hoare, No 9 F/L D. McGregor. Manager S/L R. E. Storer. Engineers F/O Harrow, F/O Whitby. *Ground Crew:* F/Sgt Hutson, Sgt Thomas, Cpl Chadburn, Cpl Fernside, Cpl Mayes, Cpl Mearns, Cpl Wood, J/T Austin, J/T Fennell, J/T Hardgreaves, J/T Howse, J/T Hurren, J/T Jones, J/T Scurr, J/T Steer, SAC Boucher, SAC Carroll, SAC Dawson, SAC Gannon, SAC Green, SAC Thomas.

1967 Leader S/L R. G. Hanna, No 2 F/L D. A. Bell, No 3 F/L F. J. Hoare, No 4 F/L P. R. Evans, No 5 F/L R. Booth, No 6 F/L H. J. D. Prince, No 7 F/L E. E. Jones. Manager F/L L. G. Willcox. Engineer F/O D. Whitby, Adjutant F/L R. Dench. *Ground Crew:* F/Sgt Hutson, C/T Watson, Sgt Thomas, Cpl Bennett, Cpl Chadburn, Cpl Fletcher, Cpl Nevard, Cpl Smith, Cpl Thomas, Cpl Thurstans, Cpl Turrell, J/T Austin, J/T Dalgleish, J/T Fennell, J/T Harris, J/T Howse, J/T McKnight, SAC Carroll, SAC Dunn, SAC Gannon, SAC Smith, SAC Stidwill.

1968 Leader S/L R. G. Hanna, No 2 F/L D. A. Bell, No 3 F/L D. A. Smith, No 4 F/L P. R. Evans, No 5 F/L F. J. Hoare, No 6 F/L R. Booth, No 7 F/L J. T. Kingsley, No 8 F/L I. C. H. Dick, No 9 F/L R. B. Duckett. Manager S/L L. G. Willcox. Engineer F/O D. Whitby, Adjutant F/L R. Dench. *Ground Crew:* C/T Watson, Sgt Souter, Sgt Thomas, Cpl Bennett, Cpl Fletcher, Cpl Nevard, Cpl Smith, Cpl Thomas, Cpl Thurstans, Cpl Turrell, J/T Austin, J/T Dalgleish, J/T Fennell, J/T Goodfellow, J/T Harding, J/T Harrington, J/T Harris, J/T Hudson, J/T Walters, SAC Bell, SAC Carroll, SAC Jones, SAC Pinkerton, SAC Stidwill.

1969 Leader S/L R. G. Hanna, No 2 F/L P. R. Evans, No 3 F/L D. A. Smith, No 4 F/L R. B. Duckett, No 5 F/L E. R. Perreaux, No 6 F/L J. T. Kingsley, No 7 F/L I. C. H. Dick, No 8 F/L J. D. Rust, No 9 S/L R. P. Dunn. Manager F/L P. Mackintosh. Engineer F/O G. E. White, Adjutant F/L R. Dench. *Ground Crew:* F/Sgt Young, C/T Loader, C/T Souter, Sgt Dicker, Sgt Fowler, Sgt Stuart, Cpl Blight, Cpl Harris, Cpl Hudson, Cpl Jones, Cpl Perrett, Cpl Sivell, Cpl Thomas, Cpl Turrell, J/T Fothergill, J/T Goodfellow, J/T Keyworth, J/T Scammell, SAC Bell, SAC Cresswell, SAC Farra, SAC Gannon, SAC Hyland, SAC Jones, SAC Pinkerton, SAC Williams.

1970 Leader S/L D. Hazell, No 2 F/L E. R. Perreaux, No 3 F/L D. A. Smith, No 4 F/L J. D. Rust, No 5 F/L J. Haddock, No 6 F/L I. C. H. Dick, No 7 F/L R. B. Duckett, No 8 F/L D. S. B. Marr, No 9 F/L R. E. Loverseed. Manager F/L P. Mackintosh. Engineer F/L G. E. White, Adjutant WO L. Ludlow. *Ground Crew:* FS Arthur, C/T Dicker, C/T Fowler, C/T Francis, C/T Souter, C/T Thomas, Sgt Blight, Sgt Turrell, Cpl Goodfellow, Cpl Jones, Cpl Scammell, Cpl Sivell, J/T Heeley, J/T Lagor, SAC Bell, SAC Cresswell, SAC Crewe, SAC Farra, SAC Frampton, SAC Gannon, SAC O'Brian.

1971   Leader S/L R. E. W. Loverseed, No 2 S/L D. S. B. Marr, No 3 F/L A. C. East, No 4 F/L W. B. Aspinall, No 5 F/L P. J. J. Day, No 6 F/L C. F. Roberts, No 7 F/L R. E. Somerville. Manager F/L K. J. Tait. Engineer F/L G. E. White, Adjutant WO L. Ludlow. *Ground Crew:* F/Sgt Fisk, C/T Dicker, C/T Fowler, C/T Souter, C/T Thomas, Sgt Baker, Sgt Stuart, Cpl Armstrong, Cpl Audley, Cpl Hudson, Cpl Jones, Cpl Lawrence, Cpl Perrett, Cpl Scammell, Cpl Webb, J/T Heeley, J/T Lagor, J/T Ruffle, SAC Bell, SAC Cresswell, SAC Frampton, SAC Gannon, SAC Goddard, SAC Howard, SAC Marsh, SAC Shorter, SAC Thompson.

1972   Leader S/L I. C. H. Dick, No 2 F/L W. B. Aspinall, No 3 F/L A. C. East, No 4 F/L R. E. Somerville, No 5 F/L K. J. Tait, No 6 F/L P. J. J. Day, No 7 F/L D. Binnie, No 8 F/L E. E. G. Girdler, No 9 F/L C. F. Roberts. Manager F/L B. Donnelly. Engineer F/L I. Brackenbury, Adjutant WO S. Wild. *Ground Crew:* F/Sgt Fisk, C/T Dicker, C/T Fowler, C/T Martin, C/T Shea, Sgt Ransom, Sgt Sampson, Cpl Armstrong, Cpl Hudson, Cpl Lawrence, Cpl Perkin-Ball, Cpl Potter, Cpl Scammell, Cpl Walton, Cpl Webb, J/T Blandford, J/T Ruffle, SAC Bell, SAC Cresswell, SAC Goddard, SAC Marsh, SAC Radge, SAC Shorter, SAC Tarte, SAC Worthington.

1973 Leader S/L I. C. H. Dick, No 2 S/L W. B. Aspinall, No 3 F/L B. Donnelly, No 4 F/L E. E. G. Girdler, No 5 F/L K. J. Tait, No 6 F/L D. Binnie, No 7 F/L R. E. Somerville, No 8 F/L D. J. Sheen, No 9 F/L P. J. J. Day. Manager F/L R. M. Joy. Engineer F/L I. Brackenbury, Adjutant WO H. E. D. Rundstrom. *Ground Crew:* F/Sgt Fisk, C/T Hosking, C/T Martin, C/T Shea, Sgt Dalgleish, Sgt Ransom, Sgt Sampson, Cpl Armstrong, Cpl Hudson, Cpl Marson, Cpl Perkin-Ball, Cpl Potter, Cpl Scammell, Cpl Walton, Cpl Webb, J/T Blandford, J/T Lee, J/T Ruffle, SAC Bell, SAC Chandler, SAC Clay, SAC Cresswell, SAC Dallison, SAC Radge, SAC Shorter, SAC Vale, SAC Worthington.

1974 Leader S/L I. C. H. Dick, No 2 F/L K. J. Tait, No 3 F/L B. Donnelly, No 4 F/L E. E. G. Girdler, No 5 F/L C. M. Phillips, No 6 F/L D. Binnie, No 7 F/L R. E. Somerville, No 8 F/L D. J. Sheen, No 9 F/L R. Eccles. Manager F/L R. M. Joy. Engineer F/L I. Brackenbury, Adjutant WO H. E. D. Rundstrom. *Ground Crew:* F/Sgt Bennett, C/T Martin, C/T Hoskins, C/T Hambrook, Sgt Dalgleish, Sgt Ransom, Sgt Sampson, Sgt Whelan, Sgt Rees, Cpl Utting, Cpl Lee, Cpl Potter, Cpl Mackinder, Cpl Marsden, J/T Lee, J/T Blandford, SAC Vale, SAC Dallison, SAC Ellis, SAC Bell, SAC Worthington, SAC Hoddy, SAC Coates, SAC Chandler.

1975 Leader S/L R. B. Duckett, No 2 F/L M. J. Phillips, No 3 F/L B. Donnelly, No 4 F/L R. Eccles, No 5 F/L J. Blackwell, No 6 F/L D. J. Sheen, No 7 F/L B. R. Hoskins No 8 F/L M. Cornwell, No 9 F/L R. S. Barber. Manager S/L A. L. Wall. Engineer F/L A. Hunt, Adjutant WO H. E. D. Rundstrom. *Ground Crew:* F/Sgt Rockett, C/T Rapley, C/T Ransom, C/T Hambrook, Sgt Dalgleish, Sgt Ryan, Sgt Brewer, Sgt Whelan, Sgt Rees, Cpl Cameron, Cpl Homewood, Cpl Kilgariff, Cpl Greenhalgh, Cpl Mackinder, Cpl Marsden, J/T Trim, SAC Dallison, SAC Noble, SAC Ellis, SAC Powell, SAC Worthington, SAC Slater, SAC Hoddy, SAC Cross, SAC Coates, SAC Edlin, SAC Branson.

1976 Leader S/L R. B. Duckett, No 2 F/L M. J. Phillips, No 3 F/L R. Eccles, No 4 F/L D. R. Carvell, No 5 F/L R. S. Barber, No 6 F/L B. R. Hoskins, No 7 F/L M. Cornwell No 8 F/L M. T. Curley, No 9 F/L N. S. Champness. Manager S/L A. L. Wall. Engineer F/L A. Hunt, Adjutant WO H. G. Thorne. *Ground Crew:* F/Sgt Rockett, C/T Rapley, C/T Hambrook, Sgt Ryan, Sgt Goodfellow, Sgt Brewer, Sgt Whelan, Sgt Rees, Sgt Kilgariff, Sgt Greenhalgh, Cpl Pugh, Cpl Cameron, Cpl McLaughlin, Cpl Homewood, Cpl Mackinder, Cpl Davies, J/T Dallison, J/T Bell, SAC Ellis, SAC Powell, SAC Ingram-Luck, SAC Hoddy, SAC Coates, SAC Everett, SAC Branson, SAC Noble.

1977 Leader S/L F. J. Hoare, No 2 F/L D. R. Carvell, No 3 F/L R. S. Barber, No 4 F/L M. J. Phillips, No 5 F/L N. S. Champness, No 6 F/L M. Cornwell, No 7 F/L M. T. Curley, No 8 F/L R. M. Thomas, No 9 F/L M. B. Stoner. Manager F/L M. B. Whitehouse. Engineer F/L A. Hunt, Adjutant WO H. G. Thorne. *Ground Crew:* F/Sgt Rockett, C/T Lipscomb, C/T Hambrook, Sgt Ryan, Sgt Goodfellow, Sgt Brewer, Sgt Fisher, Sgt Rees, Sgt Kilgariff, Cpl Cameron, Cpl Pugh, Cpl Powlesland, Cpl Mackinder, Cpl Davies, J/T Bell, J/T McLaughlin, SAC Ingram-Luck, SAC Yea, SAC Lumb, SAC Hill, SAC Everett, SAC Branson, SAC Foster, SAC Oxford.

1978 Leader S/L F. J. Hoare, No 2 F/L D. R. Carvell, No 3 F/L M. B. Stoner, No 4 F/L M. J. Phillips, No 5 F/L L. A. Grose, No 6 F/L M. T. Curley, No 7 F/L R. M. Thomas, No 8 F/L S. R. Johnson, No 9 F/L B. C. Scott. Manager S/L M. B. Whitehouse. Engineer F/L R. A. Lewis, Adjutant WO H. G. Thorne. *Ground Crew:* F/Sgt Rockett, C/T Lipscomb, Sgt Brewer, Sgt Rees, Sgt Mackinder, Sgt Leek, Sgt Lee, Sgt Powlesland, Cpl Pugh, Cpl Cameron, Cpl McLaughlin, Cpl McDonald, Cpl Kay, Cpl Wise, Cpl Davies, J/T Thomas, J/T Scullion, J/T Clarke, J/T Mathews, SAC Lumb, SAC Ingram-Luck, SAC Foster, SAC Goodwin, SAC Everett, SAC Oxford.

1979   Leader S/L B. R. Hoskins, No 2 F/L M. T. Curley, No 3 F/L B. C. Scott, No 4 F/L M. D. Howell, No 5 F/L M. B. Stoner, No 6 F/L R. M. Thomas, No 7 F/L S. R. Johnson, No 8 F/L N. J. Wharton, No 9 F/L W. Ward. Manager S/L R. Thilthorpe. Engineer F/L R. A. Lewis, Adjutant WO H. G. Thorne. *Ground Crew:* F/Sgt Rockett, C/T Lipscomb, Sgt Lee, Sgt Brewer, Sgt Dicker, Sgt Leek, Cpl Ruffle, Cpl Cameron, Cpl McLaughlin, Cpl Trim, Cpl Smale, Cpl McDonald, Cpl Dallamore, Cpl Inman, Cpl Wise, Cpl Marks, J/T Thomas, J/T Scullion, J/T Clarke, J/T Mathews, SAC Lumb, SAC Oxford, SAC Goodwin, SAC Foster, SAC Mawdsley, SAC Everett, SAC Ingram-Luck.

1980   Leader S/L B. R. Hoskins, No 2 F/L M. D. Howell, No 3 F/L W. Ward, No 4 F/L N. J. Wharton, No 5 F/L B. C. Scott, No 6 F/L R. M. Thomas, No 7 S/L S. R. Johnson, No 8 F/L B. S. Walters, No 9 F/L T. R. Watts. Manager S/L R. Thilthorpe. Engineer F/L R. A. Lewis, Adjutant WO H. G. Thorne. *Ground Crew:* WO Rockett, C/T Lipscomb, Sgt Lee, Sgt Dicker, Cpl Trim, Cpl Clarke, Cpl Inman, Cpl Ruffle, Cpl Gledhill, Cpl Sellars, Cpl Dallamore, J/T Thomas, J/T Scullion, J/T Mathews, SAC Seddon, SAC Ingram-Luck, SAC Mawdsley, SAC Newton, SAC Phelps.

1981 Leader S/L B. R. Hoskins, No 2 F/L B. S. Walters, No 3 F/L W. Ward, No 4 F/L M. H. deCourcier, No 5 F/L N. J. Wharton, No 6 F/L S. R. Johnson, No 7 F/L T. R. Watts, No 8 F/L I. J. Huzzard, No 9 F/L J. R. Myers. Manager S/L R. Thilthorpe. Engineer F/L G. M. Nisbet, Adjutant WO H. G. Thorne. *Ground Crew:* F/Sgt Harding, C/T Ellwood, Sgt Lee, Sgt Marks, Sgt Smith, Sgt Adlington, Cpl Trim, Cpl Inman, Cpl Hunter, Cpl Taylor, Cpl Bailey, Cpl Taylor, Cpl Singh, Cpl Smith, Cpl Scullion, Cpl Thomas, J/T Topham, SAC Clarke, SAC Carnell, SAC Brooks, SAC Hales, SAC Price.

1982 Leader S/L J. Blackwell, No 2 F/L B. S. Walters, No 3 F/L J. R Myers, No 4 F/L I. J. Huzzard, No 5 F/L W. Ward, No 6 F/L T. R. Watts, No 7 F/L M. H. deCourcier, No 8 F/L T. W. L. Miller, No 9 F/L P. A. Tolman. Manager S/L R. Thilthorpe. Engineer F/L G. M. Nisbet, Adjutant WO H. G. Thorne. *Ground Crew:* F/Sgt Harding, C/T Ellwood, Sgt Lee, Sgt Marks, Sgt Smith, Sgt Clinton, Sgt Freeman, Cpl Keelan, Cpl Hunter, Cpl Goodwin, Cpl Inman, Cpl Holmes, Cpl Singh, Cpl Bingham, Cpl Sparks, J/T Stevens, J/T Neale, J/T Rumming, SAC Ingram-Luck, SAC Newton, SAC Carnell, SAC Seddon, SAC Hales.

1983   Leader S/L J. Blackwell, No 2 S/L I. J. Huzzard, No 3 F/L J. R Myers, No 4 F/L T. W. L. Miller, No 5 F/L E. H. Ball, No 6 F/L M. H. deCourcier, No 7 F/L P. A. Tolman, No 8 F/L S. H. Bedford, No 9 F/L C. A. R. Hirst. Manager S/L J. E. Steenson. Engineer F/L M. E. J. Render, Adjutant WO H. G. Thorne. *Ground Crew:* F/Sgt Harding, C/T Ellwood, Sgt Lee, Sgt Smith, Sgt Marks, Cpl Singh, Cpl Inman, Cpl Stevens, Cpl Sparks, Cpl Peffers, Cpl Fitzgerald, Cpl Stevens, Cpl Keelan, Cpl Smith, Cpl Holmes, Cpl Neale, Cpl Bingham, J/T Woodley, J/T Rummings, J/T Doel, SAC Tutty, SAC Carnell, SAC Newton.

1984   Leader S/L J. Blackwell, No 2 F/L S. H. Bedford, No 3 F/L G. I. Hannam, No 4 F/L T. W. L. Miller, No 5 F/L E. H. Ball, No 6 F/L P. A. Tolman, No 7 F/L A. R. Boyens, No 8 F/L P. D. Lees, No 9 F/L A. K. Lunnon-Wood. Manager S/L J. E. Steenson. Engineer F/L M. E. J. Render, Adjutant WO D. H. A. Chubb. *Ground Crew:* F/Sgt Vaughan, C/T Ellwood, Sgt Smith, Sgt Henderson, Sgt Sturgeon, Sgt Verney, Sgt Peffers, Cpl Neale, Cpl Singh, Cpl Holmes, Cpl Clayton, Cpl Marshall, Cpl Fitzgerald, J/T Doel, J/T Elliss, J/T Sievewright, SAC Fieldhouse, SAC Taverner, SAC Tutty.

1985 Leader S/L R. M. Thomas, No 2 F/L P. D. Lees, No 3 S/L E. H. Ball, No 4 F/L S. H. Bedford, No 5 S/L G. I. Hannam, No 6 F/L A. R. Boyens, No 7 F/L A. K. Lunnon-Wood, No 8 F/L C. D. R. McIlroy, No 9 S/L A. B. Chubb. Manager S/L H. R. Ploszek. Engineer F/L M. E. J. Render, Adjutant WO D. H. A. Chubb. *Ground Crew:* F/Sgt Vaughan, C/T Fisher, Sgt Rutter, Sgt Thompson, Sgt Sturgeon, Sgt Symons, Sgt Peffers, Cpl Smee, Cpl Clayton, Cpl Fitzgerald, Cpl Ayres, Cpl Bainbridge, Cpl Constantine, Cpl Brooks, Cpl Blake, Cpl Pickford, J/T Rumming, J/T Wallace, J/T Gray, SAC Fieldhouse, SAC Sproggs, SAC Mathieson, SAC Bull, SAC Gould, SAC Archdale.

1986 Leader S/L R. M. Thomas, No 2 F/L P. D. Lees, No 3 S/L A. B. Chubb, No 4 F/L P. J. Collins, No 5 F/L G. I. Hannam, No 6 F/L A. K. Lunnon-Wood, No 7 F/L C. D. R. McIlroy, No 8 F/L D. W. Findlay, No 9 F/L A. P. Thurley. Manager S/L H. R. Ploszek. Engineer F/L J. S. Chantry, Adjutant WO H. A. Chubb. *Ground Crew:* F/Sgt Roper, C/T Fisher, C/T Rutter, Sgt Thompson, Sgt Rouse, Sgt Phillips, Cpl Ayres, Cpl Fitzgerald, Cpl Turner, Cpl Brooks, Cpl Constantine, Cpl Wallis, Cpl Pickford, Cpl Gooding, Cpl Smee, Cpl Marshall, Cpl Wallace, J/T Rumming, J/T Gray, SA Bull, SAC Fieldhouse, SAC Hall, SAC Wilson.

1987 Leader S/L R. M. Thomas, No 2 S/L P. J. Collins, No 3 F/L M. A. Carter, No 4 F/L M. J. Newbery, No 5 S/L A. B. Chubb, No 6 F/L C. D. R. McIlroy, No 7 F/L A. P. Thurley, No 8 F/L J. E. Rands, No 9 F/L G. M. Bancroft-Wilson. Manager S/L H. R. Ploszek. Engineer F/L J. S. Chantry, Adjutant WO M. R. J. Fleckney. *Ground Crew:* F/Sgt Roper, C/T Fisher, Sgt Rutter, Sgt Rouse, Sgt Brown, Sgt Barclay, Sgt Thomas, Cpl Wallace, Cpl Marshall, Cpl Gooding, Cpl Turner, Cpl Gray, Cpl Graham, Cpl Smee, Cpl Ayres, Cpl Chidley, Cpl Constantine, Cpl Wallis, J/T Chadwick, SAC Hall, SAC Mathieson, SAC Bull, SAC Fieldhouse.

1988 Leader S/L T. W. L. Miller, No 2 F/L G. M. Bancroft-Wilson, No 3 F/L D. C. Riley, No 4 S/L P. J. Collins, No 5 F/L S. W. M. Johnson, No 6 S/L A. P. Thurley, No 7 F/L J. E. Rands, No 8 S/L J. W. Glover, No 9 F/L M. A. Carter. Manager S/L H. R. Ploszek. Engineer F/L J. D. Williams, Adjutant WO M. R. J. Fleckney. *Ground Crew:* F/Sgt Roper, C/T Rutter, Sgt Rouse, Sgt Thomas, Sgt Laws, Sgt McKeown, Sgt Brown, Cpl Wallace, Cpl Graham, Cpl Gooding, Cpl Fitzgerald, Cpl Ayres, Cpl Turner, Cpl Marshall, Cpl Bayliss, Cpl Watson, Cpl Wallis, Cpl Mantle, Cpl Gray, J/T Wilson, SAC Hill, SAC Graves, SAC Fountain, SAC Bull, SAC Rich.

1989 Leader S/L T. W. L. Miller, No 2 F/L A. W. Hoy, No 3 F/L M. J. Cliff, No 4 F/L G. M. Bancroft-Wilson, No 5 F/L D. C. Riley, No 6 F/L J. E. Rands, No 7 F/L S. W. M. Johnson, No 8 S/L J. W. Glover, No 9 F/L J. M. Newton. Manager S/L A. J. Stewart. Engineer F/L J. D. Williams, Adjutant WO M. R. J. Fleckney. *Ground Crew:* F/Sgt Ellwood, C/T Rutter, Sgt McKeown, Sgt Rouse, Sgt Brown, Sgt Thomas, Sgt Laws, Cpl Mantle, Cpl Lavelle, Cpl Graham, Cpl Gray, Cpl Jones, Cpl Ayres, Cpl Chadwick, Cpl Wallis, Cpl Smee, Cpl Wallace, Cpl Bond, Cpl Taylor, J/T Wilson, J/T Watson, SAC Rich, SAC Graves, SAC Ford, SAC Bull, SAC Fountain.

SELECTING THE PILOTS
SQUADRON LEADER TIM MILLER

In January a signal is sent to all units in the Royal Air Force inviting applications. Candidates must have a fast jet background (i.e. have flown Harriers, Phantoms, Jaguars, Buccaneers or Tornados), have at least 1500 flying hours to their credit (which means they will probably have completed about two tours of duty) and have been graded 'above average' or 'exceptional' by their previous squadron commander. Usually about fifty people will apply and because of the qualifying criteria most will be in their early thirties with probably 2000 or more flying hours. The fifty or so applicants are filtered down and the Team formally interviews nine pilots, three of which will be selected for the next season.

It is taken as read that every candidate called forward for interview could do the job so far as the flying is concerned, but what is essential is that the individuals who are ultimately selected should fit in. Each member of the Team has to be able to place one hundred per cent trust in all the other members, so we are looking for level-headed, experienced pilots who are compatible (because they are going to live and work so closely together) and who are honest (because they must be ready to admit their

Opposite: Rolling 'Viggen' formation above cloud during 'early-in-the-year' practice

Below: Squadron Leader Miller, leader in the year of the Team's Silver Jubilee

(photo: Lou Peeters)

errors – and even the Leader sometimes makes them). There is no room for prima donnas nor for persons who cannot take criticism.

The Team pilots review all the applications to decide which pilots are to be invited for interview. Because the Royal Air Force is a comparatively small community it is rare for any applicant not to be known by at least one of the Team, and therefore the discussion concerning the applications will include this personal knowledge. When the list has been reduced to eight or nine, those applicants are invited to a three-day intensive interview at Scampton in March.

On the first day the applicants will fly with the Team on their training sorties, sitting in the back seat of the Hawks. Then in the evening they will be taken out in the company of both the Team members and their wives. The next day the applicants will fly again, and following that each undergoes a formal interview by the Commandant of the Central Flying School and the Team Leader in which they have to answer all sorts of questions, including the really difficult one: 'Why do you want to join the Red Arrows?' (If someone thinks being in the Red Arrows will make him special, then he is not the sort we are looking for.) The Leader reports back to the other members of the Team and they all discuss the candidates. Names are then put on a board and each Team member is asked to nominate his first, second and third choice so that everyone can see how the candidates are viewed. Eventually three are selected.

The successful pilots are advised in April and then have to wait until September before coming to Scampton. They arrive for the last two weeks of the display season and during those two weeks they fly with the Team in the back seats. This enables them to experience precisely what it is like to be 'on the road', because during that time they will participate in some

Right: Eight of the long serving Air Defence Phantoms of Strike Command now being replaced by the latest air defence system, the Tornado F.3 *(below)*

Top left: A tight line-abreast formation of the 'twice-the-speed-of-sound', 'variable-wing' interdiction/strike aircraft – IDS Tornados of No 617 Squadron. *Below left:* The incomparable Buccaneer low-level strike aircraft, and *(below)* the unique VTOL Harriers from No 4 Squadron in Germany all flown in this picture by ex-members of the Red Arrows

ten to fifteen displays and visit perhaps three or four countries. This is an extremely valuable initiation because although there are a great number of written Standard Operating Procedures with which all Red Arrows pilots have to be familiar, the actual day-to-day existence can be learned only through experiencing it.

Early in October there is the Red Arrows end-of-season Guest Night, hosted by the Team and attended by as many ex-Team members as can make it. Additionally invitations are extended to aviation personalities who have been good friends to the Team over many years, and to others who have helped particularly during the preceding twelve months. At midnight the three pilots whose three-year tour is ending become ex-Team members and the newcomers become Red Arrows. It is really a case of 'The King is Dead. Long Live the King.' I have experienced this departure myself – the Leader being a pilot who has previously been a Red Arrows member. It is a strange feeling. Although there is a great sense of achievement and you know you have had a wonderful three years, there is also a tinge of sadness. But, during your tour, you have always known that you are really only a lodger with a three-year lease. I personally believe the Team is much bigger than any individual.

After the Guest Night, the Team members who have completed the season have two weeks' leave during which time the newcomers go to RAF Valley to convert to Hawks. Then, around the end of October or the beginning of November, the Team reassembles at Scampton and the training period begins.

Opposite: Another fast jet, the Jaguar, which some of the Red Arrows have flown

TRAINING
SQUADRON LEADER TIM MILLER

Training starts with the Team Leader flying with two of the newcomers, one on each wing. The sortie is flown at 3000 feet, the height at which the first ten sorties have to be flown. This initial sortie will be made up of gentle wing-overs probably ending with a loop or two because, although the newcomers are very experienced fast-jet pilots with maybe as many as 2500 flying hours, they will never have flown formation aerobatics. In the Royal Air Force, other than with the Red Arrows, it is not legal to do so. The next sortie will be similar, with perhaps a roll, and so the training gradually builds up. Weather permitting, the Leader will be flying three sorties a day, initially with two newcomers at a time, then with the third. After the first ten sorties, the next ten are flown at 1000 feet and the next fifteen at 500 feet. Thereafter all training is at display height.

While the Leader is breaking in the newcomers, the Synchro Pair (Synchro Leader, a third-year Team member, and Synchro 2, a second-year member destined to be Synchro Leader in the following year) will be flying on their own, building up their flying relationship and confidence in each other and developing the Synchro Pair's role in what is to be the forthcoming season's display. The remaining three Team members help the Leader in the training of the newcomers. They fly in the newcomers' back seats to give guidance and advice. When the Leader wants to introduce some new manoeuvre into training, such as roll-backs, the old hands will fly to demonstrate, with the new members in the back seat, and then for the next sortie the seats will be swapped. After about six weeks the Leader will have a couple of the old hands flying with the newcomers making up a 'six ship' which can fly a half Diamond.

From the time that the training has come down to display height, every sortie will be videoed by the Team's photographer, a member of the first-line ground crew whose specific responsibility is to make video records of the Red Arrows' training and displays. He also travels to every display with the Manager.

A mid-winter portrait of a straight-and-level station-keeping exercise over the snow and ice of the spectacular Snowdonia area in North Wales

One of the difficulties in perfecting the flying of the various formations (and the changes between them) is assessing the accuracy of the pilots. The Leader has a very good idea of how steadily the aeroplanes are being flown because he watches through his mirrors, but it takes some time to master this skill. Initially the Leader must concentrate solely on flying smoothly, because this is essential if the Team is to be able to formate without difficulty.

The video record is obviously invaluable at every debrief. The Leader reviews the entire flight from his memory with the other Team members chipping in, commenting on problems, suggesting solutions to any difficulties and generally considering the performance. Then the video is run. Freeze frame will reveal in each formation whether any aircraft was even slightly out of position, and slow-motion playback will show if there was any unevenness in any change. There can be times when we spend as long as ten minutes reviewing a single frame. Even when the season has begun, the Team debriefs after every sortie and, if facilities are available, immediately views the video recording. However, sometimes, especially if the Team is travelling between displays, it may not be possible to view for a few hours. In those circumstances we debrief with the videos when we get to the hotel. In the old days the sorties used to be filmed using a 16mm black and white camera, with as much as a fortnight's delay before a print could be viewed. Videos have the great advantage of immediacy.

It should be noted that there is not a great deal of help that can be given by most people watching from the ground. Close-formation aerobatics is such a specialised aspect of aviation that, although the Team welcomes constructive criticism, there are very few people with the experience and knowledge to give it. Of course, ex-members of the Red Arrows are the exception because they fully understand the technique behind our type of flying, but there are only some eighty or so individuals who have ever flown for the Team and they are now spread around the world!

After some two and a half months of training, when the Synchro Pair will have perfected their sequence to near display standard and the Leader is satisfied that the Front Seven are flying smoothly and accurately, the two sections will be married together and the Team as a 'nine ship' will commence training.

Each year's display will be slightly different but will usually combine the same or similar formations. After twenty-five years of flying with nine aeroplanes most possible formations have been tried by the Red Arrows and only the effective ones remain in the repertoire. But each year's Team will have its preferences or may simply want some change between one

---

Early training formations rarely seen outside the immediate vicinity of the Red Arrows home base

Overleaf: The Synchro Leader (Red 6) flies low down the runway using the snow covered edge as reference, whilst his number two (Red 7 in the Team) flies in opposition

year and the next. In the 1988 display the Team rolled Wineglass, whereas for 1989 we chose to roll Delta. The two formations are similar in that both entail five aircraft flying line abreast, and both are equally difficult to fly. But the two patterns look very different to the general viewing public and consequently the alteration is appreciated by the many people who turn up to watch the Red Arrows year after year. In addition in 1989 we rolled Big Vixen, something I thought would be too difficult to fly at a consistent display standard – I was wrong.

As the nine-ship training progresses more complex formations are introduced and when the Leader feels the Team is ready he introduces the manoeuvres he wishes ultimately to include in the forthcoming season's display. He is working up to produce a twenty-minute sequence of flying which will include as many as possible of the Red Arrows' 'trademarks' and yet will ensure that there is always something happening in front of the crowd. The aim is for the show to be punchy, dynamic and fluid so that 'Little Johnnie doesn't have time to go and buy his potato chips'.

The display will be in two parts. The first, which is a nine-aircraft aerial ballet, has the whole Team flying together, always in view of the crowd. It will include one of the Red Arrows' trademarks, the Big Nine to Diamond Nine arrival loop, and will end with another: the Synchro Split from Leader's Benefit into the Cascade. Then the whole tempo of the display changes. The Synchro Pair and the Front Seven alternate 'on stage' in a powerful, exciting sequence where the Synchro Pair perform manoeuvres such as the double rolls and the opposition loop, and the Front Seven fly manoeuvres such as the Caterpillar and the Vixen Break. Subject to the weather, the display will end with all nine aeroplanes joining up in a loop to conclude with the Parasol Break.

Weather is always a problem because some of the manoeuvres such as all the loops, the Caterpillar and the Parasol Break need height (up to 5500 feet). The Team therefore prepares three displays. First there is the 'full' display for good weather, when the cloud base is above 4500 feet (or the sky is clear) and visibility is at least 3 nautical miles. This enables all loops, rolls and wing-overs to be performed without restriction. Second is the 'rolling' display, when there is a minimum cloud base of 2500 feet and visibility of 3nm. This limits flying to those manoeuvres which do not depend on height for effect and so therefore excludes loops. Finally, the 'flat' display is for the worst conditions, when cloud base is down to 1000 feet and/or visibility is only 2nm. In these circumstances the manoeuvres are limited to the display being flown in the horizontal plane.

Although the Team practises all three types of display, it also practises switching from one to another because frequently during the British summer the weather can change in minutes. The Red Arrows train to such a pitch that on the word of the Leader, the display can be switched from 'flat' to 'full' and then back again to 'flat' to take advantage of a break in the cloud cover. Or, with poor weather advancing, the Red Arrows can begin 'full', change part way through to 'rolling' and finish 'flat'.

The Team's photographer at work, videoing a practice

'Diamond Nine' is the basic formation used throughout the history of the Red Arrows. From this pattern all other formations in the repertoire of the Team have been evolved

These photographs show different angles on the beautiful smoking pattern in a looping plane as airshow spectators would see it, while overleaf is a pilot's eye view (from No 10, the Manager's aircraft) of the rear of the Team as the backswing of the 'Diamond Nine Loop' is commenced

The 'Rhombus' formation, photographed with the 1984 team, is the tightest formation flown by the Red Arrows. Only a few feet separate each aircraft

Right: The 'Heart-Loop-Cascade', where the Synchro Pair split from the main formation at the top of the loop, and, after scribing a heart shape in smoke, the main formation complete their loop and fly through the heart, breaking formation in a cascade

The 'Roll Backs', where six aircraft, in matched alternating pairs, pull out from the formation and then roll back into it as they fly down the length of the crowd line

Right: The Team Manager flanked by the Central Flying School Commandant (left) and the Air Officer Commanding (right) as they watch the display at RAF Akrotiri

Normally, by the end of February the complete Team will be flying all the formations and manoeuvres for the forthcoming season. At Scampton we have more opportunity to practise 'flat' and 'rolling' displays than 'full' ones, so in April, after a week's leave, the Team and the ground crew transfer to Cyprus.

This trip serves many purposes. Apart from enabling the Red Arrows to begin the season with a suntan, it gives the Team almost unlimited opportunities to practise full displays: three or four sorties in clear skies every day. It also gives the Team the chance to practise over the sea. About 35 per cent of displays take place at coastal sites and displaying over the sea is very different from displaying over land. If it is hazy and there is no horizon it is very difficult initially to know how high you are. Also on the wing it can be very disorientating. As the wingmen concentrate on flying in relation to the Leader, often they may not really know which way up they are. Consequently practice over the sea is invaluable.

The Cyprus trip is also the first time for the team in its widest sense, that is the ten pilots and supporting ground crew, really to work together. Once the season is under way ten selected first line engineers allocated to the Hawks will transit – i.e. travel to the bases from which displays are flown – in the back seat (these ten are known famililarly as the 'flying circus'), with the rest of the travelling ground crew transiting by Hercules. So this is the chance for the ground crew and pilots to build a good relationship. The circus engineers, with assistance from the other ground crew when appropriate, prepare the aircraft as if they were their own, so that when the Team briefing has finished the pilots can jump straight into the Hawks to find the switches set ready to start. Therefore it is very important that the necessary trust develops.

Additionally, as it is the first transit sortie of the year, it is time for the ground crew to learn about loading up the Hercules with a spare engine, spare wheels, jacks, every conceivable tool, nuts and bolts, spare radios, oxygen, nitrogen, dye, and all the other necessary bits and pieces including, of course, the pilots' golf clubs. So the trip to Cyprus is where the operation really gels.

At the end of three weeks, when the display has been perfected in all areas and the necessary approval has been given by the Air Officer Commanding and the Air Officer Commanding-in-Chief, the Team returns to Britain and, after five and a half months of intensive training, the season begins.

The five-and-four-loop-and-roll, where Red 6 (the Synchro Leader) positions his four-ship formation for a loop towards the crowd, whilst the Leader takes his section of five aircraft in a barrel roll through the centre of Red 6's loop made clear by the smoke shadows. This photograph was taken over RAF Akrotiri in 1980

Overleaf: The support Hercules carrying the Team's equipment and 1st line ground crew join up with the 1989 Leader's favourite formation – 'Big Vixen' - for a quick photo-sortie after leaving the fjords of Norway and before climbing to altitude to transit back to the UK

TEAM ORGANISATION
SQUADRON LEADER TIM MILLER

All of the Team, including the ground crew, have an important part to play in making the Red Arrows a success. There are many people who could be mentioned here but the basic structure of the Team is as follows. The Team Leader, the Officer Commanding the Red Arrows (familiarly known as the 'Boss'), is ultimately responsible but underneath him there are nine pilots and two engineering officers. Of the eight pilots who display with the Leader, there is Synchro Leader and Synchro 2 and two navigation planners, and the ninth pilot is the Team Manager (Mange), who has an administrative staff to assist him. The engineering officers are Eng 1, in charge of the first line ground crew (which includes the flying circus), and Eng 2, in charge of the second line ground crew.

The Leader is a pilot of Squadron Leader rank who has previously flown with the Red Arrows. At any one time there are very few pilots who meet these criteria and there are normally no more than two or three people qualified for the job. Furthermore, it is not a position for which one applies. One is invited and has to undergo interviews by the Air Officer Commanding and ultimately the Air Officer Commanding-in-Chief.

Leading the Team is very different from being a wingman. My first tour was 150 per cent enjoyment. My responsibility in the air was to be in the right place at the right time and to do what I was told by the Leader – sometimes easier said than done! Being Leader is not so much fun but it is more professionally satisfying. It is an opportunity for a Squadron Leader to lead in a way that has not applied in the Royal Air Force since the Second World War; to lead both on the ground and in the air, to brief and lead every single sortie and to make every decision while airborne when the pressure is on.

When you know there are some 50,000 people who have paid good money to attend an air show at which the Red Arrows are scheduled to display and the weather is deteriorating, the pressure is on to fly. But at the back of your mind you know you must look after the Team who place such trust in you. There is a fine dividing line between 'The show must go on' and 'This is silly', but you have to think ahead and this is where experience helps.

The display's final manoeuvre before landing back at the Farnborough show – 'The Parasol Break'

Left: Ready for Leader's start-up call on the R/T

Above top: Refuelling

Above middle: Turn-round check

Above: Replenishing with dye

For example, the Team was once scheduled to appear at Middle Wallop. This is an Army Air Corps show and it has become traditional for the Red Arrows to appear. It was the sort of day when many aerobatics teams would not even have bothered to get airborne: cloud base not much above 1000 feet, rain and such poor conditions that one was quite pleased even to find the airfield. But, as usual, we arrived on time and began a 'flat' display. Unbeknown to me, the display site had a very good personal address system and so during his commentary the Manager was occasionally plugging the PA into my transmissions (to which he listens throughout the display) so that the crowd could hear me giving calls to the Team: 'Apollo. Go.'; 'Smoke On. Go.' etc. The weather got worse and worse so, at the end of the first half, when normally the Synchro Pair would split, I decided to terminate the show and I transmitted, 'That's your lot, Mange. I'm calling it a day' – to the whole crowd!

It is not just the decisions in the air during the display which are the responsibility of the Leader. He has to get the Team to the display site, which can be some way from the operating airfield where the ground crew service the aircraft. It is a matter of professional pride to the Red Arrows that they always arrive on time, and that means not just within sight or sound of datum but over datum at the scheduled time, plus or minus 2 seconds. For instance, if we were to display at Guernsey at 12.30 hours, operating out of Jersey, which is 4 minutes and 56 seconds flying time away, then we would physically roll (i.e. brakes off) at precisely 12.25:04 hours.

Working out the route to a display is the responsibility of the two navigation planning officers who are invaluable to the Leader. They plan every single sortie, devising a sensible route which avoids controlled air space, danger areas, bird sanctuaries and any identifiable hazards. Then the timing is calculated working back from the required arrival time. The nav planners calculate how much fuel is required, they select suitable diversions, they obtain radio frequencies and they provide all the relevant details about the airfields to be visited. Although the nav planners may consult with the Leader before finally determining a route, it is they who ultimately produce an appropriately marked up map for each sortie (the original of which is used by the Leader with the rest of the Team having photocopies).

In addition to the maps provided for each display site (which incidentally are only ever used once because by the following year they may well be out of date) there are aerial photographs and other reports. During the winter site surveys are carried out to view the terrain and identify any particular problem areas (such as bird sanctuaries) or hazards (such as high temporary structures not indicated on aviation maps). The Leader

---

'Big Seven' bending as they line-up on the display line of the Warbirds Airshow at West Malling

Overleaf: An unusual angle of a typical seaside venue taken from 5,000 feet above the airshow datum at Weston-super-Mare as the team execute the 'Vixen Break'

Unique air-to-air close-up photographs of the
Synchro Pair as they split for their routine

and Synchro Leader will check each site survey, the Leader from the aspect of the display as a whole and the Synchro Leader with specific consideration of its relevance to his part of the display (because of his need for particular reference points and a lower minimum safe altitude). It has been known for the results of a site survey to lead to a decision by the Team to withdraw from a display for safety or environmental reasons.

The report of a site survey together with appropriate maps covering transit to the site and the display area itself (this latter map and associated aerial photograph being marked with specific details relating to the display) are part of the material placed in the file which is maintained for each display. This file also includes a military police survey report on the display area which identifies places such as hospitals, old people's homes, stud farms etc., which should not be overflown. It is the Leader's job to review these documents thoroughly, in conjunction with the latest weather report, prior to briefing the Team immediately before departure for a display sortie.

Once the Team is airborne, it is the Leader who does all the actual navigation. The nav planners assist him by taking responsibility for the VHF radio calls to air traffic control (leaving the Leader free to make the UHF radio calls which direct the Team) but it is the Leader who has to get the Team to each display on time. So it is he who adjusts the heading and airspeed at which the Team is flying so as to remain on the planned route and to maintain a ground speed of 360 knots (6 nautical miles a minute), the speed at which the nav planners have timed the sortie.

One needs about twenty minutes for the necessary concentrated consideration of maps, weather and other relevant data (such as diversion airfields, obstacles, etc.) – most of which has to be memorised – prior to the Team briefing which itself takes place thirty minutes before take-off for the display.

Life for the Team gets busy. It should be appreciated that in the middle of the season the Red Arrows sometimes fly three displays in a day, transiting between sites, sometimes involving a change of countries. As for the rest of the year, the Team's public relations responsibility is probably at its greatest during the winter. It is then that they give talks and lectures to various bodies ranging from the Royal Aeronautical Society to local branches of the Women's Institute. In addition, the Leader is frequently called upon to present awards and prizes, give interviews etc. Also in the winter there is the detailed planning for the next season including making decisions as to which invitations to display are to be accepted, from which airfields display sorties are to be operated, where the Team should stay when away from base etc. Also, as happens all year round, the Leader has the general day-to-day administration of any squadron commander. The Leader's is a very time-consuming and demanding job, but nevertheless one feels greatly privileged to be offered it.

Framed between the engines of a Catalina amphibian at the 'Fighter Meet' at North Weald

The Manager, who like the Leader is a Squadron Leader, is responsible to the Leader for all the administrative/logistic support, making sure, with the assistance of an Adjutant, that everything is in the right place at the right time. The Manager also flies the spare aircraft between display venues and he is the link man on the ground doing the commentary for all the shows. Before the season he makes all the arrangements for the Team's appearances. Once it has been agreed by the Ministry of Defence that the Team can appear at a display, the venue will be slotted into the season's programme. Detailed planning then begins. This ranges from the obvious things such as booking accommodation for overnight stops, arranging adequate catering and fixing transport, to dealing with local currencies and visas. All these details are collected together in the appropriate display files. A couple of weeks before the commencement of a trip the Manager will issue to all concerned a document detailing all relevant timings and associated facts. This document, which even includes details such as organised social events, etc., is familiarly known as a WHAM, from 'What's happening, Manager?'. WHAMs were devised by the Manager for the 1984 to 1987 seaons (Sqn Ldr Henry Ploszek) as a way to prevent the oft-repeated question from being asked too often!

As well as organising the season's displays, during the winter the Manager coordinates all the publicity material and deals with all sorts of odds and ends, such as getting the Team's red suits made and equipping the new pilots. He travels around the country visiting various display organisers, and also starts outlining the following year's timetable.

Once the season has begun it is the Manager's responsibility to be the Red Arrows' man on the spot at each display site, to commentate during the display, to handle the Team's PR and to iron out any local difficulties. He also has to be available to sort out problems if an eventuality not anticipated in the WHAM occurs. If the transport's late, the hotel poor and the restaurant has closed half an hour before we arrive, the poor Mange always takes a hit. Still, if he couldn't take a joke he shouldn't have joined!

In practice, the Manager departs from Scampton with the Team, flying the No 10 Hawk to the base from which the display sortie is to be flown (the circus member who is the Team's photographer in his back seat). If this base happens to be an airfield which is also the display site then he and video man merely vacate the aeroplane (which is then prepared as the spare aircraft) and set off for datum to carry out their respective duties. If, however, as is often the case, we have landed at an airfield from which the Team are to fly to the display site, then the Manager and the photographer have to get to the site in advance of the Red Arrows.

When such a site is an airfield, as part of the pre-season planning, the Manager will have arranged for a light aircraft (a Bulldog) to be waiting

Pulling-out of the seven-ship line-astern 'Caterpillar Loop' at Farnborough Airshow

Overleaf: As the 500th BAe 125 Corporate jet crosses the coast on its way to an American customer, the Team's Red 1 and 2 form up for an industry publicity photograph

at the operating base, which he will then fly to the display airfield, taking the photographer as passenger. Should the display site be somewhere else, such as a seafront, he will have arranged for a helicopter (normally a Gazelle) to be available for him, in which case he may well require further transport to get him to the datum point. This position has to be reached because it is there that the photographer videos the display and so reveals whether the Team performs precisely on target. The Manager also has to be at the datum point because it is there that the PA system will be situated through which he will give his commentary on the display.

In accordance with standard Team practice, the Manager plans to be at the datum point forty minutes before display time, i.e. during the time when the Leader is preparing for the pre-flight briefing. Thanks to modern technology, since the 1988 season Mange has been able to provide the Leader with an additional service. He and the Leader are now each kitted out with a Cellnet telephone so on reaching his commentary position he calls the Leader to supply up-to-the-minute information. The sort of things which are telephoned might be statements to the effect that the weather is deteriorating faster than estimated in the Met briefing; that the display is running three minutes late; that a 120-foot-high crane has been built at a location which Mange pinpoints, etc. These are invaluable data which the Leader can then pass on to the Team when, as is traditional, he gives his pre-flight briefing on the wing of Red 5's aeroplane. Why No 5? Because it's in the middle of the line!

During the next thirty minutes or so the Manager, having checked the PA arrangements, does his PR bit for the Team, talking to the public who can easily identify him because of the distinctive red flying suit. A few minutes before the display time Mange will be at his commentary position with a UHF radio tuned in to the Team's frequency. The Leader will report his progress to Mange but as the Red Arrows normally transit low level to a display, it is possible that the terrain over which they are flying will cut out the transmission. This is where the Team's immaculate timing comes into play. Even if he has not heard a position report from the Leader on his radio, ten seconds before the due display time the Manager can announce, 'Ladies and Gentlemen, the Royal Air Force Aerobatic Team, the Red Arrows', confident that, provided he has spoken at the correct speed, as his voice dies away over the PA system the Team will roar in over the crowd and the show will be under way.

From then on the Manager will commentate to the crowd, drawing attention to relevant parts of the display, alerting the spectators to changes so that they get the most out of each manoeuvre. Throughout this time Mange will be listening to the Leader, linking the transmission to the PA system if he thinks it appropriate. In this way he is aware if the Leader

High level transits are usually flown at between 35/40,000 feet in two sections. Here the back four led by the Synchro Leader are photographed from the Manager's aircraft

Overleaf: The latest BAe 146 airliner leading the Red Arrows in a specially arranged formation over the Jet Provosts of CFS at Scampton in April 1989

has to change the display because of a lowering cloud base – for example the display may be changed from 'full' to 'rolling' to 'flat'. While the display is on it is only the Leader who makes any decision on what is to be flown, where, how and when.

Once the display is over and the courtesies have been duly completed, Mange and video man will get into whatever is the relevant means of transport to return so that the photographer's video can be incorporated in the debrief. In the meantime the Hawks will be replenished with fuel, smoke oil (derv) and smoke dyes in readiness for the next sortie.

Normally the Team will fly two displays a day, sometimes three, and up to three transit sorties a day. In these circumstances if Mange and video man have to transit on between displays without returning to the operating base, it may not be until the evening that the Team will be able to view the video. Traditionally we all pile into Red 7's room (Red 7 is always responsible for videos) and debrief before dinner. On average it takes forty minutes to debrief each display. On a three-display day, dinner is often late!

While the Team is debriefing Mange is checking that everything is proceeding in accordance with the WHAM. He confirms the next day's arrangements, verifying hotel bookings (he does all checking in and out for the Team), transport etc.

In addition to the ten pilots, the Red Arrows Team includes the ground crew, a close-knit group with challenging, interesting work whose very nature means that its members travel widely. If they get to the top positions, they fly with the Arrows as back-seaters. The ground crew is made up of two officers (Eng 1 and Eng 2) and some fifty other engineers, all of whom have volunteered for the position. The second line, whose officer in charge is Eng 2, are the airmen who spend most of their time at Scampton doing the really heavy repair work and servicing. It is their responsibility to take out the engines and strip down the aircraft during the winter servicing. They rarely travel away from base, although two or three will normally transit with the Team on an overnight trip. If a major engineering difficulty occurs when the Team is 'on the road', Eng 2 will muster the necessary men and equipment and they will hasten to the rescue.

The first line ground crew, of whom there are about twenty-six including their officer in charge, Eng 1, are the men who always travel with the Team. Ten of their number, the flying circus (all of whom will have served at least a year on the first line), transit in the back seats of the Hawks. The job of these ground crew is to handle basic day-to-day servicing, to refuel the aircraft and replenish them with derv and dyes. Also, during the winter, some 50 per cent of their number work with the second line on the 'deep strip servicing' which is carried out on each of the Red Arrows' Hawks in readiness for the forthcoming season.

Positioning a helicopter to capture a picture of the British Army Air Corp helicopters and the Red Arrows in one mixed formation, later sold to raise funds for the Army Flying Museum at Middle Wallop

Practising the 'Apollo' formation

The pilots and ground crew really come together when they deploy to Cyprus for the final stage of training. The ground crew is made up of airmen with various trades: there are electricians; airframe, air communications, air radar, flight systems and engine/propulsion technicians; and armourers (responsible for ejection seat and canopy explosive systems). Each man is a specialist who knows his own job, but each is cross-trained to have a knowledge of other trades and all work very closely together because there are times when team work, not specialisation, is necessary. In many ways it is a very similar operation to a Formula One motor racing team. For example, frequently wheel changes have to be carried out at very short notice.

The flying circus includes Eng 1 and covers all trades. Competition to be a back-seater is fierce and only the very best technicians get selected. The circus leader, normally a Sergeant, is responsible for the other engineers and traditionally he flies in the Team Leader's back seat.

When Mange issues a WHAM, the circus leader takes it apart to produce his own document for the circus detailing the matters of relevance to them. This is primarily a breakdown of timing so that each airman knows precisely how many minutes are available between each touch-down and take-off for all necessary turn-round servicing. But it also includes precisely how much fuel is required for each sortie to ensure that appropriate refuelling arrangements are made.

It is Eng 1, the officer in charge of the first line, who has the main ground crew responsibility. It is his job to ensure that all work is completed on time, and he is the one to get the engineers to work at an appropriate time in advance of the pilots' first sortie. He also has to get the aircraft rolled out and prepared each day. When the Team is on the road in a Herc-supported push, he is responsible for all the engineering and its quality control; he is in charge of all the travelling ground crew including the circus and the circus leader.

On reaching the operating base there is normally little more than sixty minutes before take-off on a display sortie. During this time Mange and video man transit to the display site, while the Leader does his final preparation and then briefs the Team. As for the circus, they set about any necessary servicing. This entails refuelling and loading with derv and dye, and carrying out the detailed pre-flight checks of all systems. Between displays the ground crew handle the refuelling etc., as previously mentioned, together with any necessary minor servicing such as wheel changes. At the end of the day, and sometimes even overnight, more major servicing will be carried out.

As will be shown in the remainder of this book, although everyone knows his particular job and the way his responsibilities enable the Red Arrows to maintain their reputation for reliability and professionalism – to live up to the squadron motto 'Eclat' (excellence) – it is teamwork and adaptability which is the key to their success.

'Rhombus' looping over Farnborough

A WEEKEND IN THE LIFE OF...
SQUADRON LEADER TIM MILLER

In the following pages there is a description of a display weekend showing how the various parts of the Team, in its widest sense, work together to ensure that the general public see a polished flying performance at the time expected. It is based upon an actual weekend during the twenty-fifth anniversary display season.

The text is an expanded WHAM of a three and a half day weekend which included six displays (one each at Shawbury, Lee on Solent and Humberside, and three at Fairford) and two fly-pasts (the more important one over Troon). Each column notes the times at which anything specific happened from the start of activity on Friday morning until the end of the trip on the following Monday. The first column reproduces the WHAM and the two other columns detail the activities of the Red Arrow pilots (including Mange) and those of the support (Red Arrow engineers/technicians, Hercules crew and others) separately, which it is hoped will clarify how the work of the two parts interlock.

The various hiccups and the way that they were overcome are entirely typical of the way in which the Red Arrows operate.

A frigate of the Royal Navy acts as datum for the display at Dartmouth in 1987

WHAM	AIRCREW
FRIDAY	**FRIDAY**

<table>
<tr><td>09.00 Ground crew in.</td><td></td></tr>
</table>

WHAM	AIRCREW
10.00 Reds in.	10.00 All ten pilots in. Leader's planning meeting.
10.15 Met brief.	10.15 Met brief in crew room (report on weather for transit to Shawbury; expected weather for transit to Hurn; transit to, display at and transit from Fairford back to Hurn).
	10.20 Leader is given map prepared by the relevant route planning officer (Reds 4 and 5 plan all transits and displays throughout the season) and discusses with the officer (Red 4) timings, frequencies, heights, fuel, weather, diversion airfields, danger areas, Royal Flight movements, arrival procedures, instrument patterns, circuit directions and parking arrangements for the transit.
11.00 Transit brief.	11.00 Leader gives briefing for 14 minute 10 second transit to all ten pilots in the briefing room based upon the discussion with the planning officer, all pilots having their own copies of the route map.
	11.18 Pilots walk to aircraft and strap in.
	11.20 Pilots carry out R/T check and start engines, Leader calling the start-up etc.
	11.23 Hawks taxi.
	11.28 Pre take-off checks.
	11.29 Leader calls tower on VHF for take-off clearance.

SUPPORT

09.00 Ground crew in.
Having collected from 2nd line ground crew records
on aircraft to be flown 1st line ground crew
commence before flight composite check of Hawks,
one engineer per two aircraft cleaning and checking
airframe. Separate teams check and top up as
necessary, gases, hydraulics, tyres, fuel, dye and
derv.

09.45 Before flight check complete.
Roll-out of Hawks from hangar commences under
control of towing team. When aircraft in place on
tarmac, earth lead fixed and undercarriage locks
removed, team responsible for each aircraft signs off
documents confirming completion of all checks.

10.00 Eng 1 and Flight Sergeant attend planning
meeting.

Rolling out

10.20 Roll-out complete.
Coffee break.

10.45 Walk-round check of each Hawk carried out
by team different from that which carried out before
flight check. Earth, pitot head cover, chocks
removed. All pressures checked again, all surfaces
rechecked, ejector seat and oxygen systems
checked.

11.13 'Travelling circus' into Hawks.

11.18 Ground crew strap pilots into Hawks. When
engines have started, verify to pilots (by means of
hand signals) satisfactory operation of airbrakes etc.

11.21 Fire crews and technicians withdraw.

11.23 Ground crew marshal Hawks to taxiway.

Met. brief

Transit brief

WHAM	AIRCREW
FRIDAY	FRIDAY

AIRCREW

FRIDAY

11.29:20   Leader calls Reds on their special Red Arrow UHF frequency: 'Smoke, Lights on. Go'; 'Power'; 'Parking Brakes'. (Which is to have all systems armed and set for take-off.)

11.29:47   Leader calls 'Reds . . .

11.29:48   . . . Rolling . . .

11.29:50   Reds depart Scampton.

11.29:50   . . . Now' and the pilots take off, climb to their normal transit height of 500 ft and form up in Standard Battle formation – which is two sections of five aircraft, each section with the aircraft flying approximately 50 yds apart, the second section, led by Red 6, being approximately 1500 yds behind Leader's section. (Red 4 and Red 5, who fly in the front section, sometimes climb higher than 500 ft for effective VHF communication, rejoining the loose formation as appropriate.) The Hawks cruise at 6 nm per minute (360 kts).

11.30:30   While all pilots remain on the Red Arrows' discreet UHF frequency, Red 4 calls Waddington on VHF and asks for radar information.

11.32   Red 5 calls East Midlands on VHF to advise on transit details (during transits the route planning officers alternate the ATC calls, leaving the Leader free to concentrate on navigation and to give instructions to the Reds on UHF although he also listens out on all VHF transmissions). On this occasion East Midlands advises intense gliding activity 5 nm ahead. Leader alters course accordingly to avoid this area. Throughout the transit all pilots keep a lookout for other aircraft.

11.35   Herc arrives Scampton.

11.37   Red 4 calls Shawbury Approach for the runway in use, QFE (airfield pressure), wind, cloud and visibility.

11.37:30   Leader, having decided on basis of this information on a flat, left, right break arrival, briefs the team on UHF.

11.42:30   Red 5 calls Shawbury Tower for clearance to join the airfield zone and for landing clearance.

11.43   Leader calls the Team into close formation (from Standard Battle). Red 6 acknowledges for the second section.

Loading the Hercules

Overleaf: Arrival break

11.35   Herc lands at Scampton.

11.40   Loading of Herc by loading team under
supervision of Herc loadmaster and UK Mobile Air
Movements Squadron (UK MAMS) controller begins.

WHAM	AIRCREW

11.45   Reds arrive Shawbury.

11.45:00   The Team breaks left and right and lands at Shawbury. When Red 10 has confirmed he has landed and come to a full stop, Leader calls 'Lights off. Go' and pilots carry out individual and close-down checks. The pilots park the Hawks at dispersal in one straight line.

11.48   Display organiser greets Leader and advises him and other pilots of display arrangements, e.g. refreshment facilities, transport arrangements around display site, etc. Manager checks with display organiser on commentary position and arrangements for gaining access to it.
Planning officer for Shawbury display (Red 4) reports to air traffic for display and met information. This is to verify that display slot time remains as pre-planned (if it has changed he has appropriately to amend the documents to be supplied to Leader), to check on arrangements for taxiing in and out, and to obtain latest weather details for wind, cloudbase and visibility to enable Leader to decide whether a full, rolling or flat display is to be flown.
While Red 4 is obtaining this information, Leader and Synchro Lead (Red 6) are looking at the aerial photographs of the display obtained on the site survey and the display map prepared by Red 4 and comparing it with the actual site, e.g. verifying anticipated hazards are as expected and noting unexpected hazards (such as a newly erected mast). Once Red 4 has reported back with display details, Leader prepares for the display briefing and Red 6 with the other Synchro Pair member (Red 7) brief together for their part of the display.
During this time the pilots without designated duties are mingling with the public, handing out brochures, stickers, etc., giving autographs, i.e. general public relations. Leader, Mange, Synchro Pair and display planning officer join in this PR exercise when free.
All pilots make time for a coffee and a snack; it will be some time before there will be a chance for further refreshment.

SUPPORT

11.48   At Shawbury, circus commence turn-round
composite check, one engineer per aircraft. Aircraft
are cleaned up, fatigue meters noted, airframes
checked for damage, search for defects made.

12.30   Lunch break at Shawbury.
Back at Scampton the loading of the Herc continues
and it is discovered that there is a mechanical fault
on the Landrover used for towing gas, derv and dye
wagons etc. Back-up Landrover is obtained but,
because of Herc transport rules, battery has to be
removed and enclosed in heavy duty pvc before

Left: Spit 'n' polish
Top: The Team line up
Middle: Checking jet pipe
Above: Public relations

13.25   Display brief.

13.25   Leader gives display brief on the wing of No 5 (the middle aircraft) commencing with a short debrief of the uneventful transit from Scampton.

13.45   Mange sets off for commentary position.

13.50   Pilots walk to their aircraft and pre take-off procedure (as before the transit sortie) commences.

13.55   Hawks taxi for display take-off. Mange begins his commentary with a general introduction.

13.58   Pilots take off and depart to form up in Big Nine for the display arrival. Mange continues his introduction which, depending on circumstances, can be of as much as 10 minutes' or as little as 30 seconds' duration.

13.59:52   Mange announces, 'It gives me great pleasure to introduce the Royal Air Force Aerobatic Team, the Red Arrows.' He gets his timing right so that the roar of the arrival is heard as his voice dies away.

14.00   Reds display Shawbury.

14.00–14.20   The Red Arrows display at Shawbury.

SUPPORT

refitting (to prevent risk of acid spillage in the event of a bumpy flight) – a 20-minute job.

It is also noted that, efficiently, Landrover has full tank of fuel, UK MAMS requirement is no more than 75% full – again to avoid spillage (not just in flight but during loading and unloading when the vehicle is winched aboard up a 45-degree ramp). Excess fuel has to be siphoned off (another 20-minute job).

13.15   At Shawbury walk-round check carried out (as before transit from Scampton) for all ten aircraft.

Display brief on No 5 wing

13.45   Back-seater of No 10 (video man) to video position.

13.50   Remaining circus strap pilots into Hawks, carry out final walk-round and, on start-up, verify to pilots operation of airbrakes etc. Fire crews provided by RAF Shawbury personnel.

13.55   Circus marshal Hawks to taxiway.

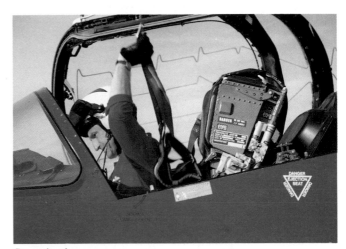

Strapping-in

14.00   Circus watch display.

14.10   Ground crew at Scampton finish loading Herc.

If all goes smoothly loading the Herc from scratch takes 2 hours but because of the Landrover problem this took 2½ hours. Loading once 'on the road' takes less time because not all items get unloaded at each stop-over.

Refuelling

123

14.21   Reds land after a successful full display.

SUPPORT

14.21   Hawks having landed at Shawbury, circus marshal them to parking positions, receive pilots' report on any defects and commence turn-round check; checking the airframe, outlets and intakes, switches and gauges. Aircraft are refuelled (dye and derv having to wait until Hurn as they are carried in the Herc). Lack of dye and derv help turn-round which normally takes one hour.

Left: Final break
Above: Parking

125

WHAM	AIRCREW
FRIDAY	FRIDAY

AIRCREW — FRIDAY

14.25   Red 4 delivers to Leader route map for transit to Hurn and after discussion about the route sets off for air traffic to confirm departure slot time and transit weather details (updating the information obtained earlier) which he reports back to Leader who is preparing for transit briefing.

14.45   Mange rejoins Reds having handled some additional PR after completion of his commentary. All pilots try to grab a quick coffee.

WHAM — FRIDAY

14.50   Herc departs Scampton.

14.55   Transit brief.

15.22:45   Reds depart Shawbury.

15.30   Herc arrives Hurn.

AIRCREW — FRIDAY

14.55   Transit brief on wing of No 5.

15.15   Pilots to aircraft for pre take-off procedure as usual.

15.20   All ten Hawks taxi for transit take-off.

15.22:45   The Team takes off from Shawbury. This transit is of 22 minutes 15 seconds' duration (hence the apparently odd departure time which guarantees arrival at the due time). Because it is a longer transit and the route is through some controlled airspace zones Reds 4 and 5 between them have to contact six different frequencies en route in addition to the tower and approach frequencies at departure and arrival airfields.

15.34   Manager (Red 10) peels off from the second section of the Standard Battle formation and takes up heading for Fairford.

126

SUPPORT

14.40   Herc captain and co-pilot start up Herc engines and with their engineering officer, navigator and ground engineer complete their own start-up check.

14.45   Video man at Shawbury delivers video cassette of Shawbury display to Red 7 (Red 7 being responsible for video).

14.50   Herc takes off from Scampton and the ground crew in the back 'enjoy' the flight to Hurn jammed into the Herc with the gas, derv and dye wagons, Landrover and all the spares and tools which make the Red Arrows self-sufficient when staying away from base. This of course includes the suitcases of the pilots and the flight bags of the ground crew.

15.10   At Shawbury, back-seaters to Reds 1–9 into Hawks for transit to Hurn, video man into No 10 for transit to Fairford.

15.30   Herc lands at Hurn. Ground crew start unloading in readiness for arrival of Hawks.

Top: Herc takes off
Above: 'Enjoying' the Herc ride

127

WHAM	AIRCREW
FRIDAY	FRIDAY

WHAM — FRIDAY

15.38   Red 10 lands Fairford.

15.45   Reds 1–9 arrive Hurn.

AIRCREW — FRIDAY

15.38   Manager lands at Fairford and, having made preliminary contact with the display organiser, assists in the turn-round check of No 10, there being only 20 minutes for this and refuelling to be completed.

15.45   Reds 1–9 land at Hurn.

15.50   Red 5 presents Leader with a prepared map for the transits to and from Fairford – a rather indirect, roughly circular route, because of air traffic restrictions. (Both the route to and the route from Fairford – which differ – are about 90 nm long. A crow flying at Hawk speed would fly only some 65 nm, straight over Boscombe Down and a number of designated danger areas!) Red 5 also provides Leader with the map for the display at Fairford as the transit and display are to be flown as one sortie. After discussing the route and display area with Leader, Red 5 then goes to Hurn tower to obtain met information and transit departure and return details. Meanwhile Mange sets off with the PR kit for the Fairford control tower to meet up with the display organiser.

16.00   Leader at Hurn is preparing for his briefing with Synchro Lead while Mange at Fairford is checking with the display organiser that the display slot time has not been changed and pre-notified datum has not been moved. Mange also gets weather information. He next moves to his commentary position which in this case is near datum and checks the display site against the aerial photograph produced on the site survey.

16.15   Mange returns to his aircraft where all turn-round checks have been completed and signs off final paperwork. Mange then briefs video man on the position from which he is to video the display.

16.20   Mange at Fairford calls Leader at Hurn on Cellnet and advises that the display is running on time, gives weather update, confirms that display line is clearly marked with dayglo markers and advises that there is a tethered balloon 300 yds crowd right (a hazard to be avoided) and a bright blue and white marquee 50 yds right of datum (a pinpointing advantage).
Mange and video man grab a quick coffee.

SUPPORT

15.45   At Fairford video man is working on turn-round of No 10.

15.50   Turn-round check of Hawks Nos 1–9 is under way including refuelling and reloading with dye and derv.

Above: Dye team with wagon
Top right: Red 10 lands
Middle right: Replenishing with dye
Right: Control tower

WHAM	AIRCREW

FRIDAY	FRIDAY

16.30   Display brief.

16.30   Leader briefs the Team for the transit and display. Transit to Fairford (duration 13 minutes 21 seconds) is straightforward, all have copies of the route map so all that is needed is a weather update and a reminder of hazards to be avoided en route and of diversion airfields in case of emergencies. Leader warns that 2 minutes out of Fairford he will put the Team into Big Nine formation if, as presently seems likely, they are to fly a full display, or into Nine Arrow formation if the display is to be flat or rolling or if he has still not made up his mind.

Leader then briefs the display incorporating the information telephoned by Mange. As for all displays this briefing covers the weather, hazards (pylons shown on the display map and Mange's balloon), diversions and a run-through of the manoeuvres to be flown in the context of the display site. At Shawbury all could see the site at which they were to fly; on this occasion they brief from the maps and photographs. Leader next briefs the end of the display and join up for transit back to Hurn. He briefs three end of display options (for different weather conditions). Leader ends by briefing the transit back to Hurn.

Although this is extremely detailed the briefing takes no longer than the usual 20 minutes.

While Leader has been briefing the Team, at Fairford Mange (supported by video man where appropriate) is handling PR.

16.58   Pilots walk to aircraft.

17.00   Start-up.

17.03   Hawks taxi.

17.06:39   Hawks take off for Fairford.

17.07   Mange to commentary position to check display still on time (so as to confirm this fact to Leader) and to ensure slot is still available.

17.13   Mange begins his introduction.

17.18   Weather information obtained from Fairford Approach by Red 5 having confirmed clear skies and good visibility, Leader calls Team into Big Nine formation.

Leader preparing for display brief

6.50   Turn-round check complete including all paperwork.

6.58   Circus help strap in pilots.

7.00   Start-up checks.

7.03   Ground crew and Herc crew enjoy tea break.

7.07   Video man at Fairford to video position.

Hawks roll

WHAM	AIRCREW
FRIDAY	FRIDAY
	17.19:52 Mange announces, 'It gives me great pleasure to introduce the Royal Air Force Aerobatic Team, the Red Arrows.'
17.20 Reds display Fairford.	17.20 The Team arrives in Big Nine pulling up into a loop and change into Diamond.
	17.38 The display, again full, is successful, spot on datum thanks to Mange's marquee, ends with a join-up loop and Spaghetti Break and the Team forms up and heads for Hurn. Mange collects video man and heads back to his aircraft into which the camera pack and depleted PR kit are reloaded.
17.50 Reds recover Hurn.	17.50 Reds land at Hurn with Red 6 experiencing a minor birdstrike near the airfield.
	18.00 Reds depart for hotel in minibus.
	18.10 Reds arrive at hotel, have quick drink, then move to a conference room with video machine which has been transported in the Herc. Shawbury display debrief commences with Leader giving a summary of his view of it (largely seen in his mirrors) then the video is viewed using freeze frame to dissect formations.
	18.15 Manager takes off from Fairford.
18.35 Manager recovers Hurn.	18.35 Manager lands at Hurn to be met by Eng 1.
	18.40 Manager departs for hotel with Eng 1 and the Team's luggage in the Landrover which has travelled on the Herc.

SUPPORT

17.55   At Hurn ground crew begin after-flight check of the Hawks, which is the same as the turn-round check but, in addition, includes taking readings from the fatigue counters and low cycle fatigue meters. Refuelling is carried out and re-derving and re-dyeing. The birdstrike to No 6 has fortunately caused minimal damage. (Had the damage been major the ground crew would have worked on, through the night if necessary.) After-flight check takes about an hour and ends with the aircraft secured and covered with canopies carried in the Herc as it was known no hangar space would be provided.

Left: Manager commentating on 'Gear Down Pass'
Above: ... with 'Synchro Goose'

18.10   Video man at Fairford into No 10.

18.35   Video man hands over video of Fairford display to Mange then starts on after-flight check of No 10.

Securing the canopy

WHAM	AIRCREW

FRIDAY	FRIDAY

18.50   Mange arrives at hotel and into conference room just as Shawbury debriefing is ending. Mange delivers video of the Fairford display.

18.55   As the Team begins to view the Fairford video the Manager handles the booking in of all pilots and engineers, checking arrangements for meals, etc.

19.40   Reds emerge from debriefing to collect their room keys and head for their showers.

20.30   Dinner for those Team members without social engagements (one goes out to dinner with his mother-in-law).

SATURDAY	SATURDAY

10.50   Engineers' bags and bills.

11.00   Engineers depart hotel.

10.50   Mange collects room keys from engineers to check them out of hotel.

11.40   Reds' bags and bills.

11.45   Reds depart hotel.

11.40   Reds report to hotel reception with suitcases and room keys. Mange completes checking out from hotel.

11.45   Reds depart hotel for airfield.

11.55   Reds arrive airfield. Red 4 gives Leader map for transits and display at Lee on Solent, discusses details then goes to tower to obtain weather information and confirm departure arrangements which he reports back to Leader.

134

SUPPORT

Video debriefing

19.30   After-flight check of all ten Hawks having been completed and dye and derv wagons etc. having been reloaded on the Herc, engineers and Herc crew on coach for drive to hotel.

Above: After-flight check
Below: Before-flight check

SATURDAY

10.50   Engineers and Herc crew report to hotel reception with bags and room keys.

11.00   Engineers and Herc crew board coach for transit to airfield.

11.10   Some ground crew commence the airframe checking part of the composite before-flight check of the ten Hawks while others are unloading Herc so gas, hydraulics, dye and derv and tyre teams can do their bit in due course. Herc crew assist with unloading by providing power to lower ramp.

11.15   Gazelle helicopter leaves Shawbury.

11.45   Composite before-flight check ends; all systems are topped up, paperwork has been completed. Coffee/lunch break.

WHAM	AIRCREW
SATURDAY	SATURDAY

<table>
<tr><td></td><td>12.05   Leader and Synchro Pair consider Lee on Solent display, reviewing map, aerial photographs and site survey. Leader briefs Mange on details to be checked when he reaches naval airfield, HMS Daedalus (Lee on Solent), from which he and the public will view the display.</td></tr>
<tr><td>12.15   Gazelle arrives Hurn.</td><td></td></tr>
<tr><td></td><td>12.25   Manager, carrying PR kit, boards Gazelle.</td></tr>
<tr><td>12.30   Manager departs Hurn.</td><td>12.30   Gazelle takes off for HMS Daedalus.</td></tr>
<tr><td>12.45   Manager arrives Daedalus.</td><td>12.45   Gazelle arrives at HMS Daedalus. Mange is met by display organiser and after exchange of courtesies Mange proceeds to check out display site with particular reference to points briefed by Leader and Synchro Pair.</td></tr>
<tr><td>12.50   Display brief.</td><td>12.50   Display briefing commences at Hurn. As for previous day's display at Fairford the Lee on Solent display is to be flown as one sortie.</td></tr>
<tr><td></td><td>13.00   Mange calls Leader on Cellnet and reports that on his flight into Daedalus he experienced rain, a cloudbase of only 100 ft and visibility of 2 nm but that the weather now seems to be clearing from the west. He also reports that there are a lot of seagulls crowd left. Leader incorporates this into his briefing and, as Mange's on-site report coupled with met report obtained by Red 4 confirms poor conditions, briefs for a flat show arriving in Nine Arrow formation and ending with a Vixen Break. Leader also briefs full option in case the weather clears.</td></tr>
<tr><td></td><td>13.05   Mange having completed his report gets a snack.</td></tr>
<tr><td></td><td>13.18   Reds into Hawks at Hurn.</td></tr>
<tr><td></td><td>13.20   Start-up. Mange to commentary position at Daedalus.</td></tr>
<tr><td></td><td>13.23   Hawks taxi.</td></tr>
</table>

SUPPORT

Manager and videoman take off

12.15　Gazelle arrives Hurn.

12.25　Video man, carrying video camera pack, boards Gazelle.

12.30　Gazelle takes off for HMS *Daedalus*. Ground crew supervised by Herc loadmaster and UK MAMS controller start loading Herc with items which will not be required for turn-round check.

12.45　Gazelle arrives at HMS *Daedalus*.

Preparing to strap in

12.50　Walk-round check of all ten Hawks commences at Hurn. At *Daedalus*, Gazelle pilot concentrates on turn-round check of the helicopter and video man gets himself a snack.

13.20　Video man at *Daedalus* to video position while ground crew at Hurn assist with start-up.

Marshalling

WHAM	AIRCREW

13.26 Reds depart Hurn.

13.26 Hawks take off.
Mange begins his commentary.

13.32:52 Mange announces, 'It gives me great pleasure to introduce the Royal Air Force Aerobatic Team, the Red Arrows' but his last words are drowned by the arrival of the Team in Nine Arrow formation one second early!

13.32:59 Reds display Lee on Solent.

13.32:59–13.50:59 The Red Arrows display (flat) at Lee on Solent.

SUPPORT

13.26 No 10 aircraft not having been required for display use is defuelled by ground crew so as to reduce its weight to be the same as Nos 1–9 for transit to Fairford.

Below: Part of flat display
Right: 'Nine Arrow' arrival over tower

WHAM	AIRCREW

|

14.00   Reds recover Hurn.

14.00   The Hawks land back at Hurn after an uneventful transit. Mange boards Gazelle which then takes off for Hurn.

14.05   Red 5 presents to Leader map for transit to Fairford. This differs from previous day's transit because of commitment to incorporate a fly-past over a charity fete at Waddock Cross. The route is therefore extended to some 120 nm (17 minutes and 50 seconds' flying time). After discussion about the transit Red 5 proceeds to obtain met report and departure details for Leader.

14.15   Manager recovers Hurn.

14.15   Mange lands at Hurn and reports to Leader on the display at Lee on Solent as viewed from *Daedalus*.

14.35   Transit brief.

14.35   Transit brief for all ten pilots.

14.54   Pilots to Hawks.

14.56   Start-up. Pilots verify for each other the efficacy of operation of airbrakes etc. (e.g. Red 1 watches movement of No 2's controls while Red 2 watches movement of No 1's, etc.)

14.59   Hawks taxi.

15.02:10   Reds (plus circus) depart Hurn.

15.02:10   Hawks take off for transit to Fairford flying as usual in Standard Battle formation with Reds 4 and 5 making air traffic calls on VHF while Leader maintains contact with Team on the Red Arrows' special UHF frequency.

15.05   Herc departs Hurn.

15.06:30   Leader calls the Team into Mange formation (Big Vixen with Manager positioned behind Leader).

15.07   Reds 1–10 fly past Waddock Cross.

15.07:20   Leader calls team back into Standard Battle formation for remainder of transit.

SUPPORT

14.00   Hawks 1–9 having landed, turn-round check commences excluding re-derving and re-dyeing because of shortage of time (due to specific, unalterable arrival slot at Fairford). As each piece of equipment is finished with it is loaded on the Herc.

Loading the Herc

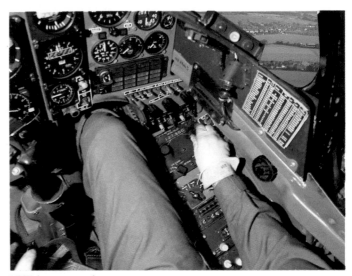
VHF frequency change

14.15   Gazelle having landed at Hurn video man delivers video of Lee on Solent display to Red 7.

14.30   Gazelle departs to return to Shawbury.

14.50   Circus including video man into Hawks, all other ground crew except Flight Sergeant and Chief Technician into the Herc.

14.57   Final engineers board Herc which starts up.

15.00   Herc taxis.

15.05   Herc takes off from Hurn.

Low-level transit

141

WHAM	AIRCREW
SATURDAY	SATURDAY
15.20 Reds arrive Fairford.	15.20 Reds arrive at Fairford.
	15.25 Red 5 gives Leader map for display at Fairford. He then goes to tower to obtain relevant display information and weather (which has improved since the morning) to report back to Leader. Leader prepares for display brief. All pilots do some general PR.
15.35 Herc arrives Fairford.	
16.00 Reds to hospitality chalet.	16.00 Reds to a hospitality chalet for tea. (The Team has invitations to a number of chalets at Fairford for both PR and social purposes, but their programme is so tight that there is only time for one to be visited.)
17.00 Display brief.	17.00 Display brief. As cloud base is now at 2500 ft and visibility 3 nm Leader briefs for a rolling display with the possibility of changing to flat if cloudbase lowers.
	17.30 Mange to commentary position.
	17.32 Pilots to Hawks.
	17.34 Start-up.
	17.37 Hawks taxi for display take-off position. Mange begins commentary.
	17.40 Hawks take off and form up in Nine Arrow for display arrival.
17.40 Reds display Fairford.	17.40–17.59 The Red Arrows display (rolling) at Fairford ending with a Vixen Break.
	18.00 Reds land at Fairford following a successful show.

SUPPORT

15.20   Reds 1–10 having landed at Fairford, circus start turn-round check.

15.35   Herc lands at Fairford. Unloading begins with dye and derv wagon coming off first to enable dye team to re-dye and re-derv Hawks 1–9.

16.20   Turn-round check complete. Tea break for engineers and Herc crew.

17.10   Walk-round check.

17.32   Video man to video position.

17.34   Start-up.

18.00   Hawks having landed, after-flight check begins. Back-seater to No 3 notices damaged tyre. Wheel change performed, which takes 20 minutes because the heat of the axle compared with the chill of the new wheel makes fitting difficult. (A wheel change can be and often is carried out when there are only the back-seaters around because on a 'circus push' a wheel change carrier containing spare wheel and tools is carried in No 1 and a jack is carried in No 3.)

Above: Autographing
Below: Herc taxis in

Unloading

WHAM	AIRCREW

WHAM

SATURDAY

18.05   IAT photocall.

AIRCREW

SATURDAY

18.05   Reds join other display pilots for a photocall arranged by the display organisers.

18.30   Reds transfer to a briefing room provided by display organiser and debrief Lee on Solent and Fairford displays.

19.45   Mange and the luggage depart for hotel (in Swindon) in the Landrover and Reds 1–9 depart for hotel in minibus but although it is more than 1½ hours since the end of the flying display, traffic is still very bad because the Team has to leave the airfield through the same gate as the general public. (The Red Arrows try to avoid airshow traffic jams whenever possible. On one trip to Norway, where the display was flown from an airfield at the end of a fjord, the Manager organised a police launch to transfer the pilots to town to enable them to arrive punctually at an official function.)

20.45   Reds arrive at hotel and retire to their rooms once Mange has checked them in.

21.30   Dinner at hotel. Rest of evening (!) at leisure.

SUNDAY

07.00   (approx) Engineers depart to reach Fairford by 8.30.

07.30   (approx) Reds depart hotel.

08.30   Display participants' brief.

09.25   Display brief.

SUNDAY

06.30   Breakfast.

07.00   Pilots leave hotel for Fairford to beat the airshow addicts who get on the road early.

08.30   Team attends display participants' briefing.

09.15   Red 5, having given Leader map for display (as before), gets weather report, which is good, and confirms display details.

09.25   Display brief for full show.

09.45   Mange to commentary position.

SUPPORT

18.30   Video man breaks off from after-flight check of No 10 to deliver video cassette of Fairford display to Red 7.

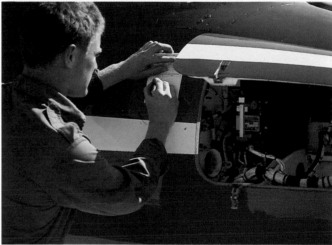

20.00   Having completed after-flight checks and secured equipment on Herc, engineers and Herc crew depart for Swindon in minibus.

20.50   Engineers and Herc crew reach hotel.

21.30   Dinner at hotel.

SUNDAY

06.30   Breakfast.

07.00   Engineers and Herc crew leave hotel for Fairford in minibus.

08.15   Having reached airfield ground crew begin composite before-flight check.

09.15   Walk-round check begins.

After-flight checks

<table>
<thead>
<tr><th>WHAM</th><th>AIRCREW</th></tr>
</thead>
<tbody>
<tr><td>SUNDAY</td><td>SUNDAY</td></tr>
</tbody>
</table>

	09.52 Pilots to Hawks. Mange commences his introduction, being able to give his full 10-minute version since the Team is to open this day's flying.
	09.54 Start-up.
	09.57 Hawks taxi.
	10.00 Hawks take off and form into Big Nine for display arrival.
10.01 Reds display Fairford.	10.01–10.19 The Red Arrows display (full) at Fairford.
	10.20 Reds land back at Fairford.
	10.25 Red 4 presents Leader with map for transit to Scampton and after drawing attention to salient points, goes to obtain weather update (CAVOK – good) for Leader and departure clearance. All pilots grab a coffee and do some general PR.
	11.25 Transit brief for all ten pilots. Route (24 minutes' flying time) is indirect because of need to avoid Birmingham and East Midlands control zones.
	11.52 Pilots to Hawks.
	11.54 Start-up.
	11.57 Hawks taxi.
12.00 Reds (plus circus) depart Fairford.	12.00 Hawks take off for Scampton.
12.05 Herc departs Fairford.	
12.24 Reds arrive Scampton.	12.24 Hawks land at Scampton.
	12.30 Red 5 presents Leader with map for transit to and from Humberside (a circular route) and for display at Humberside. Leader and Synchro Lead discuss the sortie then Red 5 goes to collect weather report (still CAVOK). Leader and Synchro Lead brief Mange on points to check at Humberside.

SUPPORT

9.52   Video man to video position.

9.54   Start-up.

0.20   Hawks having landed, turn-round check
begins including refuelling, re-dyeing and re-derving.
As use of each piece of equipment ends it is
appropriately loaded on the Herc.

0.25   Video man delivers video cassette to Red 7.

1.50   Circus into Hawks, all other engineers
except Flight Sergeant and Chief Technician into
Herc.

1.54   Remaining engineers into Herc as its pre-
flight check is being completed.

1.57   Herc starts up.

2.00   Herc taxis.

2.05   Herc departs Fairford.

2.24   Hawks having landed at Scampton, turn-
round check begins.

Part of full display
Overleaf: Forming up for display arrival

WHAM	AIRCREW
SUNDAY	SUNDAY
	12.35 Mange to Bulldog. Reds to briefing room to debrief Fairford display and transit, while enjoying a snack.
	12.40 Mange starts up Bulldog.
	12.43 Bulldog taxis.
12.45 Herc arrives Scampton.	
12.50 Manager departs Scampton.	12.50 Bulldog takes off for Humberside and Mange transits using his own transit route map.
13.00 Manager arrives Humberside.	13.00 Bulldog lands at Humberside. Mange exchanges courtesies with display organiser and then checks out display site.
	13.10 Mange reports on Cellnet to Leader advising that display site was not easy to spot when flying in but no changes have been made to site as surveyed. Mange grabs a coffee and snack then embarks on usual PR.
13.15 Display brief.	13.15 Transit and display brief (for an 8-minute transit out, a full display and a 5-minute transit back).
	13.40 Pilots to Hawks.
	13.42 Start-up. Red 8 experiences a problem with his engine so vacates No 8 and takes Mange's aircraft (No 10) which is spare.
	13.43 Red 8 starts up spare aircraft.
	13.45:30 Hawks start to taxi (30 seconds late).
	13.50 Mange to commentary position.
13.52 Reds depart Scampton.	13.52 Hawks take off for Humberside.
	13.55 Mange begins his introduction.

SUPPORT

2.35   Video man to Bulldog, leaving other circus members to turn round No 10.

2.45   Herc lands at Scampton and engineers join in urn-round of Hawks while loading team unloads verything from the Herc (which takes only about 30 ninutes).

Manager takes off

3.10   Video man at Humberside joins Mange for uick snack and then helps with PR.

3.42   Red 8's problem justifies preparation of all en Hawks.

3.43   Red 8 is assisted in his start-up check by his ack-seater and the Chief Technician.

3.44   Other ground crew with Eng 1 are already warming over No 8 to identify cause of engine roblem so as to commence repair if appropriate.

Examining the engine intake

3.50   As the Red Arrows transit and display, the round crew continue their check of No 8. (It proves) have a minor fault to its air conditioning which is asily rectified.)

3.55   Video man to video position.

WHAM	AIRCREW
SUNDAY	SUNDAY
	13.59:52 Mange announces 'It gives me great pleasure to introduce the Royal Air Force Aerobatic Team, the Red Arrows.'
14.00 Reds display Humberside.	14.00 The Red Arrows arrive in Big Nine formation.
	14.18 The Red Arrows depart Humberside after a successful full display.
14.23 Reds recover Scampton.	14.23 Reds land at Scampton.
	14.30 Red 4 gives map for transit from Scampton to Prestwick to Leader, discusses it and then goes to check on weather (still CAVOK). Manager starts up Bulldog at Humberside.
	14.40 Manager departs Humberside while Leader is preparing for transit brief and other pilots are having a coffee.
14.50 Manager recovers Scampton.	14.50 Manager lands Bulldog at Scampton.
15.00 Transit brief. Herc departs Scampton.	15.00 Transit brief for all ten pilots.
	15.15 Pilots to Hawks for start-up. (No problems this time which is a good thing as all ten aircraft are needed for the transit. There is an eleventh aircraft for use in emergencies which is maintained at Scampton ready for use and as such is rolled out from the hangar with the other ten whenever the Reds are departing from Scampton. This facility is, of course, not available 'on the road'.)
15.25 Reds depart Scampton.	15.25 Hawks take off from Scampton for an uneventful transit.
16.00 Reds arrive Prestwick.	16.00 Hawks land at Prestwick after individual straight-in approaches so as to avoid noise at the British Open Golf Championship at nearby Troon.
	16.05 Red 5 presents Leader with map for fly-past at Troon and transit to Fairford, outlines details and goes to check weather. He advises ATC that Leader will report to discuss departure details.

SUPPORT

14.23   Hawks having landed back at Scampton, turn-round check commences including refuelling and, for the last time this weekend, refilling with derv and dye. No 8's back-seater works on No 10 as Red 8 has flown that aircraft.

14.50   Video man delivers video of Humberside display to Red 7 then goes to join in turn-round check.

15.00   Herc departs for Lyneham.

15.10   Circus into Hawks.

15.25   After departure of Hawks, remainder of 1st line ground crew revert to normal Scampton duties.

16.00   Hawks having landed at Prestwick, circus begin turn-round check of all ten aircraft including refuelling.

Top: Arrival in 'Big Nine'
Above: Finish with 'Parasol'

WHAM	AIRCREW
SUNDAY	SUNDAY
16.15 Transit and fly-past brief.	16.15 Fly-past and transit brief.
16.25 Manager departs Prestwick.	16.25 Mange sets off for Troon (2 miles from Prestwick) on the back of a police motorcycle. The Team moves to the Apron Supervisor's office to debrief Humberside display.
	16.30 Mange arrives at Royal Troon. There then follows a period of waiting. The Reds and Mange, 2 miles apart, watch the golf. Mange is able to enjoy the real thing but the Reds, still in the Apron Supervisor's office, have to make do with television. Mange and Leader make intermittent contact via Cellnet. All are waiting for the end of the Championship because the intention is for a fly-past to coincide with the trophy presentation ceremony. The trouble is that golfers do not play to time and as it happens three tie so that there has to be a play-off to determine the winner. Leader takes time to visit the tower to discuss the problem of nine aircraft leaving an international airport at short notice, bearing in mind that the complete Red Arrows Team gets airborne in less time than most airliners take to taxi 500 yds. ATC agree that all possible steps will be taken to provide an appropriate take-off slot.
	19.18 The final putt has been sunk and, as Mange has agreed with the Championship organisers the time interval between this moment and the presentation, he calls Leader on Cellnet to say fly-past required at 19.40. Leader alerts ATC.
	19.32 Pilots to Hawks.
	19.33 Start-up.
	19.35 Hawks taxi for display take-off.

SUPPORT

17.00 Tea break, which initially was expected to last for no more than 15 minutes, extends and extends and extends, although all ten circus know that for nine of them it will end with a frantic rush.

19.20 Scramble!

19.30 After speedy walk-round check back-seaters to Reds 1–9 are in their respective aircraft, No 8 being operational again.

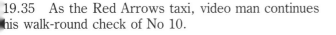

Top: Reds taxi
Above: Reds take off

19.35 As the Red Arrows taxi, video man continues his walk-round check of No 10.

155

WHAM	AIRCREW
SUNDAY	SUNDAY
A/R Reds depart Prestwick to fly past Troon and arrive Fairford 45 minutes later.	19.38 ATC having given requested clearance, Hawks take off and form into Big Vixen.
	19.40 The Red Arrows fly past Royal Troon.
	19.40:15 Reds turn on to heading for Fairford, Leader calling them into Standard Battle formation. The transit is almost direct but, because of its distance, flying time is 41 minutes 55 seconds. During the flight Reds 4 and 5 between them have to contact ten different frequencies as well as approach and tower frequencies at both departure and arrival airfields.
ASAP Manager departs Troon for Prestwick.	19.41 Mange calls Fairford on Cellnet to advise of the Team's and his own ETA for ATC and helicopter transfer purposes! He remounts the police motorcycle to be ferried back to Prestwick. Even a bike has a bit of trouble getting through the traffic.
	20.00 Mange taxis.
ASAP Manager departs Prestwick to arrive Fairford approx. 45 minutes after Reds.	20.03 Mange takes off for transit to Fairford.
	20.22 Reds 1–9 land at Fairford.
	20.27 Reds 1–9 into Chinook helicopter.
ASAP Reds 1–9 depart Fairford for South Cerney.	20.30 Reds take off in Chinook for South Cerney.
	20.40 Chinook lands at South Cerney and delivers the Team to a special party arranged for it as part of the Red Arrows' anniversary celebrations.
	20.45 Mange lands at Fairford.
	20.49 Mange into Bell Jetranger helicopter.
ASAP Manager and Eng 1 depart Fairford for South Cerney.	20.50 Jetranger takes off for South Cerney.
	21.00 Jetranger lands at South Cerney and Mange joins the party.

SUPPORT

Chinook lands

19.55   Video man gets into No 10's back seat.

20.20   Chinook pilot at Fairford commences pre-flight checks.

20.22   Reds 1–9 having landed at Fairford, circus commence after-flight check.

20.30   Chinook takes off for South Cerney.

20.40   Chinook pilot lands helicopter at South Cerney and joins the party.

20.45   Mange having landed, Bell Jetranger pilot commences his pre-flight checks while video man starts after-flight check on No 10.

20.49   Eng 1, back-seater to Red 9, into Jetranger.

20.50   Jetranger takes off.

21.00   Jetranger pilot, having landed at South Cerney, accompanies Eng 1 to the party.

Jetranger takes off

WHAM	AIRCREW

WHAM

AIRCREW

SUNDAY	**SUNDAY**

21.15 Formal presentations to the Red Arrows commence. Thanks to the golfers this is some two hours later than had been hoped, which does not accord with the Team's normal practice of being on time plus or minus no more than 2 seconds. But the British Open is a special event in the sporting calendar and the Team are all keen golfers, golf being one of the few sports which they are permitted to play during their tours of duty (the risk of injury from other games being too great).
Road transport conveys the Team back to their hotel in Swindon at the end of the evening.

MONDAY	**MONDAY**

08.00 Engineers' bags and bills.

08.50 Engineers depart hotel.

09.20 Reds' bags and bills. | 09.20 Reds report to hotel reception for Mange to check them out.

09.30 Reds depart hotel. | 09.30 Reds depart hotel in minibus for Fairford.

10.00 Reds arrive at Fairford.
Red 4 gives Leader map for transit to Scampton (as used on previous day) and goes to get weather report (good) and departure details.

10.40 Transit brief. | 10.40 Transit brief.

11.04 Pilots to Hawks.

11.07 Hawks taxi.

11.10 Reds depart Fairford. | 11.10 Hawks take off for Scampton.

11.34 Hawks arrive back at Scampton. | 11.34 Hawks land at Scampton.
Once post-flight duties are completed all pilots attack their in-trays and Reds 2–9 start preparation for the next display.

12.00 Reds 25th anniversary meeting. | 12.00 Leader and Mange to meeting re 25th anniversary . . .

SUPPORT

21.45   Back-seaters to Reds 1–8 and video man, having completed after-flight check of all ten aircraft, depart for hotel by minibus (at least by this time of night the traffic has cleared).

22.15   The nine engineers reach hotel. Rest of evening at leisure.

MONDAY

08.40   Circus report to reception for check-out.

08.50   Circus depart hotel in minibus.

09.20   Circus reach airfield and commence before-flight check.

09.30   1st line engineers other than circus report into Scampton for general duties.

11.00   Circus into Hawks.

11.34   Hawks having arrived at Scampton, circus with other 1st line engineers commence after-flight check.

12.35   Having completed after-flight check, ground crew revert to normal Scampton duties.

A welcome home from Leader's children

End of trip and after-flight checks again

159

The Squadron Badge of the
Royal Air Force Aerobatic Team
incorporating a pattern of arrowheads
in the Diamond Nine formation
with the Squadron Motto 'ECLAT'
which, when translated, means
brilliant or shining
success